The Coppages

Journey of Faith

Helping People Navigate 50 Key Obstacles to Christianity

Dr. Brent Strawsburg

Journey of Faith: Helping People Navigate 50 Key Obstacles to Christianity

Published By: Apologetics Canada Publishing
Abbotsford, BC
Canada

ISBN-13: 978-1539632382

Dedication

This book is dedicated to my dad, Floyd Strawsburg. He's a 91-year old World War II veteran, retired school teacher and pastor. He's been teaching the Bible and loving his family his entire life. He has supported me through every step of my spiritual journey. This book is a by-product of his love and encouragement in my life.

With all my love.

ACKNOWLEDGMENTS

As I travel in Southern California and throughout the country, people come up to me and ask thoughtful and penetrating questions. It's these wonderful moments of listening and sharing that compelled me to write *Journey of Faith*.

I would like to thank my dear wife Cheri who has been tremendously patient as I've spent countless long days researching, writing, and editing my book. For 35 years, she has been a faithful partner in God's calling on my life.

I would like to thank two long-time friends who have supported and encouraged me through very difficult seasons in my life. I would not be the person I am without their steadfast friendship. Rick Mastroianni, college friend from the 80's, challenged me in the formative stages of writing this book. His big picture viewpoint, in-depth thinking, and gracious input were essential in shaping the direction of *Journey of Faith*. Bob Gremel, confidant and friend from my previous church read every single page of my book and suggested necessary changes that can only come from a clear thinker and a devoted friend. Thanks to both of you!

I would like to thank a special friend, Eric MacLeod for designing the cover. His creativity, attention to detail, and commitment to excellence was a blessing. I would like to thank my two wonderful editors, Emily Kazmierski and Carol Fast who assisted me in the time consuming process of writing a book.

I would also like to thank all the friends who allowed me to integrate their personal story into the pages of *Journey of Faith*. You were honest in our discussions and selfless with your time. You jumped at the opportunity to help me write a book that connects with the real life faith journey faced by our friends inside and outside the church.

In His Grace,

Brent

TABLE OF CONTENTS

FOREWORD

"*Journey of Faith* comes from the pen of a man who is very well-educated and informed about current cultural issues and doubts about Christianity, and who has had decades of ministry working with people on these topics. Dr. Strawsburg brings these gifts to the table and has identified 50 of the most important obstacles people inside and outside of the church have with Christianity.

Journey of Faith provides us with an immensely practical and timely approach to communicating the gospel in today's skeptical climate. The book strikes the right balance between the academic and theological rigor necessary for the topic, and the pastoral compassion and guidance required for the timid faithful. Dr. Strawsburg equips us with a passionate defense of the gospel that seeks to rescue captive hearts, not win abstract arguments.

The questions raised are relevant and the answers provided distill the best apologetic thinking into readable, practical guidance for those who want to provide a defense for their hope in Christ.

Convincing and fair-minded answers to these issues are presented briefly and illustrated with real-life conversations. And the topics are arranged in a user friendly way. *Journey of Faith* is one of the best resource books for practical Christian apologetics that I have seen, and every parent, pastor, and Jesus-follower should have it ready and available on his or her shelf."

JP Moreland, Distinguished Professor of Philosophy
Talbot School of Theology, Biola University
Author of *Love Your God With All Your Mind: The Role of Reason in the Life of the Soul*

INTRODUCTION

God has placed every Christian on a unique journey of faith. We've been asked by God to embrace the truth of the Christian faith throughout every season of life. Whether we face good times or bad; easy or hard; success or failure—God invites us to place our trust in Him. The Scriptures continually emphasize the importance of faith:

- We are to live by faith, not by sight (2 Corinthians 5:7).
- It is impossible to please God without faith (Hebrews 11:6).
- We are encouraged to keep the faith from the beginning to the end (2 Timothy 4:7).
- We are to defend the Christian faith (Jude 3).

A life of faith is a never-ending dance with questions and answers that, if we allow them to, leads us deeper and deeper into the heart of God. Challenges to our faith come with the territory, and mysteriously, can actually deepen and enrich our intimacy with Jesus, the "author and finisher" of our faith. At a single moment in time, the Christian can be broadsided by issues, ideas, questions, and perspectives that hinder our journey of faith. Sometimes we and those we care about ask difficult questions that expose underlying doubts about God's nature. Is he really good? Is he really powerful enough to come through for me? Is he just?

The modern-day Christian faces even greater challenges because in our social media-driven world we are bombarded by questions. It might be a question from a family member or friend. It may be a question pointed at you from a skeptic. It also may be a question that is never asked—it simply comes to mind because of personal doubts or uncertainties. Unfortunately, it could be an unanswered question that continues to impede the progress of our spiritual journey of faith. Dr. William Lane Craig—arguably this generation's most well-known Christian apologist and philosopher hits the nail on the head:

> One of the most dangerous threats to young Christians is an honest question left unanswered. . . . I've had multiple friends tell me that their beliefs began to crumble when they voiced sincere questions to a pastor or family member and were essentially told, 'You just need

> to have more faith.'. . . . It's not enough anymore to just read Bible stories to our kids. They need doctrine, and they need apologetics.[1]

Jesus was no stranger to difficult questions. Throughout His ministry, Jesus was peppered by the questions of a skeptical audience. His miracles, teachings, priorities, and interpretations of the Law were regularly challenged. Each of these questions were designed to upend Jesus' pledge to completely follow the will of God. However, Jesus either answered the questions or responded in a way that helped people process the truth behind their faith.

We live in a skeptical culture where answers are not merely desirable—they are necessary! That's why I am writing *Journey of Faith: Helping People Navigate 50 Key Obstacles to Christianity*. The purpose of this book is to give brief answers to 50 key obstacles that attempt to derail the progress of our faith. Many of these questions threaten to undermine or detract the Christian from their pursuit of God's will for their lives. My previous book only focused on ten issues, but as we all realize, there are many other questions that serve as obstacles in our Christian journey.

Journey of Faith is unique in several powerful ways:

First, most chapters are limited to four to five pages. In a busy world, many Christians don't always have the time or the inclination to read an entire book or a very long chapter on each of these compelling issues. They want answers that they can easily get their heads around. As we continue on our spiritual journey we don't always need to read an entire book to stay on the right path. Sometimes we simply need a few well-timed and insightful words to redirect our focus and perspective.

Second, *Journey of Faith* is also written so that every chapter contains illustrations or conversations that reflect real faith experiences of Christians and skeptics alike. *Journey of Faith* is written to be a mirror that reflects the same kind of obstacles that you and I face. As you read

---

[1] William Lane Craig, https://wellspentjourney.wordpress.com/tag/william-lane-craig/

each chapter you will be able to envision having clear and meaningful conversations with skeptics and seekers alike.

Third, *Journey of Faith* is a resource guide. It's a book where 50 vital and tough questions are placed in ten easy-to-find categories. Remember, the questions that attempt to derail our faith don't all come at the same time. Often, they come uninvited into our lives without any rhyme or reason. In those moments, it's important that a person can use *Journey of Faith* as a resource.

Finally, *Journey of Faith* wants to make the subject matter of each chapter as accessible as possible. At the end of each chapter, I've added one or two sentence summaries entitled *Timeless Talking Points for a Culture that Texts.* Whether we like it or not many of our conversations have been reduced to talking points. Whether it is a post on Facebook, a quick question at dinner or a break at work, it's vital that the Christian know how to deflect criticism or respond to the objections of a friend. In an era of short and easy messages, it's important that Christians have the ability to communicate the truth to these tough questions in very short statements. *Journey of Faith* provides helpful tools so that we as believers can have more meaningful conversations about our Christian faith in a gracious and non-judgmental fashion.

In His Grace,

Brent

Dr. Brent Strawsburg

The Gospel (Good News) of Jesus Christ

The gospel of Jesus Christ is the single greatest message in the history of humanity. French Christian Philosopher Blaise Pascal described the gospel as irresistible. Billy Graham has traveled throughout the world preaching one single message—the gospel. Unfortunately, the concept of the gospel has been distorted over time. Webster's Dictionary defines the gospel as either "the teachings of the Christian religion or any one of the first four books of the Christian Bible that tell of the life of Jesus Christ." [2] Although these are accurate descriptions; they are not complete. Timothy Keller, pastor and intellectual, describes the gospel this way:

> The Greek term "gospel" (ev-angelion) distinguished the Christian message from that of other religions. An "ev-angel" was news of a great historical event, such as a victory in war or the ascension of a new king that changed the listeners' condition and required a response from the listener. So the gospel is news of what God has

[2] Webster's Dictionary

done to reach us. It is not advice about what we must do to reach God.[3]

Of course, the good news of the message about the death and resurrection of Jesus is that it has the potential to change human lives. Every person who is a follower of Jesus Christ has a unique story of how the historical event of Christ dying on the cross has shaped and transformed their life. Christ did not merely step into history to make a statement about His greatness—although the claims of Christ are absolutely unique among religions. Christ stepped into history to transform our present and our future. In other words, we are part of the story. We are a dynamic example of how Jesus of Nazareth continues to impact the lives of everyday people.

Answers for each of the questions in this section will provide the tools for Christians to better understand and respond regarding the most important truth that we've ever been given. Because this truth is of utmost importance, it's vital that we know how to explain its message with clarity and in a way that connects with our family and friends. When we do, it shines a light upon the change God can make in their own life. After all, the gospel is the story of the single greatest event in the history of humanity—God came in human flesh to die for the sins of humanity. If we are willing to acknowledge our sins and place our trust in His death and resurrection, it can reunite us with God, provide us hope for life after death, instill a sense of fulfillment, and give us the deepest joy imaginable.

---

[3] Timothy Keller, The Meaning of the Gospel—Tim Keller in *The Gospel in Action* (http://extendingthekingdom.org/?page_id=17)

Question 1

How Do We Explain the Gospel to People in a Skeptical Age?

Imagine if someone from North Korea came to your house and asked you to explain the Super Bowl, the Internet, and democracy. Where would you start? How do you explain the modern world to a citizen of a nation that has been kept in the dark for the last 50 years? Would you get mad at them for not understanding or for questioning whether anything you say is true? Of course not!

Christians have a similar challenge when attempting to explain the gospel to people who have been thoroughly immersed in a skeptical culture. The truths of the Christian faith look very different to the person looking at the church from outside the building. Think about it. Christians believe our faith is exciting and life-changing. Non-Christians think it is dull and restraining. Christians embrace the idea that Jesus has forgiven our sins. Non-Christians either question "what is sin?" or "why do I need forgiveness?" Christians scratch their head and wonder why everyone doesn't believe in Jesus. Non-Christians believe that faith is comparable to believing in Santa Claus or the Easter Bunny.

In this skeptical age, as we explain the Christian faith we must also defend it. Slowly, but surely, we need to remove the obstacles in front of our family and friends. One of the more helpful ways to explain the content of the Christian gospel is to help a person connect with the universal needs of people. Think about how these felt-need descriptions might better point people to the importance of the Christian faith:

- Satisfaction—people are hungry and thirsty for something that really satisfies. Jesus presented Himself as the one who could provide a constant source of genuine refreshment (John 10:10). Tragically, people try to fill the vacuum or dissatisfaction in their lives by another relationship, career, or wealth. The simple reality is that the presence of sin prevents people from experiencing the presence of God in the greatest way possible.
- Intimacy—people are either lonely or afraid of being alone. The gospel reminds us that we were created by God to experience

genuine fellowship with our Creator. The loneliness we feel in life stems from that initial alienation from God.

- Forgiveness—the human situation is a perpetual example that something is broken morally. Everyone experiences guilt for their choices, attitudes, and inner thoughts. Rather than addressing the cause of their guilt, many people attempt to ignore it or rationalize it away.
- Hope—our world is filled with despair, whether it stems from world situations, personal sickness, or hardship. When faced with the prospect of physical death, most people are struck by an intense sense of hopelessness. However, the gospel assures people who choose to believe that there is eternal life in heaven after we physically die.
- Purpose—an increasing number of people experience a profound sense of aimlessness. We don't have a clear set of guidelines or direction without God. God is seeking every lost person in the world in an attempt to reveal His purpose for our lives.

Second, a Christian should be able to use a Biblical passage (John 3:3 or John 3:16), a theological term (salvation, adoption, or reconciliation), or a personal experience, to explain the essence of the good news about Jesus Christ. This doesn't need to be long. The good news of Christ can be explained in thirty seconds. There is tremendous power in clearly explaining how the historical events of Christ (His crucifixion and resurrection) changed the direction of your life. Look at two examples suggested by Alister McGrath, famous English apologist, that may help you envision how to express the gospel in thirty seconds:

> In one of his letters, Paul talks about "being reconciled to God in Christ". That's a great summary of what the gospel is all about. It's about being restored to a friendship with God who has been offended. It's about Jesus making possible a new relationship with God which makes life worth living. And that's just what I found.[4]

---

[4] Alister E. McGrath, *Explaining Your Faith* (Baker Books; Grand Rapids, 1995), 31.

> Jesus once described himself as the "bread of life". Well, I realized that I was hungry, looking for something which would give meaning and purpose to my life. And I found in Jesus someone who could satisfy that hunger, and give me new life. And I've never looked back.[5]

Recently, a young millennial Christian by the name of John told me how he would communicate the gospel. It was clear and concise. Listen to his description:

> God created the world because He wanted to have an everlasting friendship with people. However, because of people's sin and indifference to Him, we could never live with Him in the perfect place called heaven. Fortunately, God sent His own Son to die on the cross for our sins. He did this so that we could live with Him forever. All we must do is to admit and repent of our sinfulness and believe that the sacrifice of Christ on the cross is sufficient to save us—nothing else.

TIMELESS TRUTHS FOR A CULTURE THAT TEXTS

The arrival of Jesus Christ into the world is good news because He has the ability to satisfy our deepest and most profound needs—both in this life and the next!

---

[5] Alister E. McGrath, *Explaining Your Faith*, 31.

Question 2
What's Unique about Christianity?

In the business world, companies are always trying to show how their products or services are unique from all their competitors. Whether you are looking online, watching a commercial, or walking into a store, you will be surrounded by attempts to promote their uniqueness. Here are some of the more common talking points:

- Largest Selection: Home Depot and Lowes provide the largest selection of home improvement items.
- Superior Customer Service: Kinko's and Jamba Juice greet everyone who walks in the door. Apple stores track the service of all customers in their store by handheld iPads.
- Convenience: Amazon offers free 2-day shipping on eligible items for its Amazon Prime customers.
- Price: Target and Walmart continually offer low price deals in an attempt to connect with thrifty shoppers.

In the religious world, Christianity claims it is unique among all religions. Jesus of Nazareth made one of the most astonishing statements in the history of mankind when he claimed that He was the unique path to the God of the universe (John 14:6). Those words spoken 2000 years ago stand in stark contrast to the modern world of the 21st century. Most everyone will tolerate some kind of religious belief as long as you don't cross the line and begin saying that your set of beliefs are right and other religions are wrong. Famous Jewish rabbi Schumley Boteach put it this way:

> I am absolutely against any religion that says that one faith is superior to another. I don't see how that is anything different than spiritual racism. It's a way of saying that we are closer to God than you, and that's what leads to hatred.[6]

---

[6] Schumley Boteach in Lee Strobel, *The Case for Faith* (Zondervan; Grand Rapids, 2000), 145.

If we are going to connect with our unchurched friends, we have to provide more evidence than simply quoting the wonderful Scriptures (John 14:6; 1 Timothy 2:5; Acts 4:12) that teach us that Christianity is the true story of God's intervention in the human story. We have to make a compelling case that there is something intrinsic to the Christian faith that places it head and shoulders above all other faiths.

It's vital that everyone recognize that the talking points of our culture stating "all religions are the same" and "all religions are equally true" are simply not accurate. Islam and Buddhism are different on every single component of their beliefs. Christianity and Islam are factually opposed on whether or not Jesus Christ was crucified. One of these two major religions must be historically wrong—they can't both be right. If all religions are not equally true, then it is absolutely necessary for people to investigate which religious worldview is most unique and accurate.

First, any religion can claim to be the only way to God, but Jesus Christ, the founder of Christianity, made extraordinary claims about His identity that makes Christianity unique among all the world religions:

- He claimed to be the Son of God—literally God in the flesh (John 8:58; John 10:30).
- He claimed to be the only way to God (John 14:6; John 8:24).
- He claimed that people can't fix their sinfulness by their own efforts (John 5:14, 22).
- He claimed to be God's sacrifice when He died on the cross (John 3:16).
- He fulfilled over 350 prophecies from the Old Testament (Isaiah 7:14; Isaiah 53; Micah 5:2).
- He was supernaturally raised from the dead and seen by over 500 people as proof of His claims (1 Corinthians 15:3-8).

As remarkable as Jesus was in His compassion, miraculous powers, extraordinary wisdom, and ethical greatness, the ultimate difference between Jesus of Nazareth and any other prophet or religious leader is His essential identity. Jesus was someone fundamentally different than anyone who has ever walked this planet. He was God in the flesh. His job was to give all of humanity a sample of God. McGrath expresses it with his distinctive clarity and insight:

> Jesus' uniqueness is, for the Christian, ultimately grounded in who he was, rather than what he said and did. In other words, Christians have always tended to regard Jesus' teaching and lifestyle as of importance because of who they knew him to be, rather than because of what this teaching and lifestyle were in themselves. . . . For traditional Christianity, the incarnation [God in human flesh] demonstrates that God has come among us as one of us, addressing us and calling us personally. . . . If the idea of the incarnation is abandoned, we are left with the picture of a Jewish rabbi, distant in time, whose teaching and lifestyle may have singled him out in his own day, but who has little relevance in ours.[7]

Second, Jesus' supernatural proof through His resurrection from the dead is unique from all other religions. None of the other founders of the major religions claimed that they would come back from the dead. History itself points to the reality that Jesus came back to life after people witnessed His public death (I Corinthians 15:3-8). This supernatural act separates the Christian faith from other religious faiths.

Third, the fundamental claims of Christianity are distinctly different from other world religions. Christians believe that Jesus died on the cross for the sins of mankind while Muslims claim that event never happened. Christians believe that the universe was brought into existence at a finite point in history—Hinduism denies this reality. Christians believe that God has a triune nature (God as three in one) and that He came to earth in the person of Jesus of Nazareth.

Christianity asserts that a person's sins must be removed solely by the sacrifice of Christ on the cross. It claims that the only way to gain reconciliation with God is through Christ. Quite to the contrary, Islam teaches that Allah is free to pardon sin at his discretion. Muslims believe there is no need for someone's substitutionary death. Buddhism focuses entirely on the need to attain compassion or inner peace. It has no intention of leading people into a personal relationship with God. It's

---

[7] Alister E. McGrath, *Understanding the Trinity* (Grand Rapids: Zondervan, 1988), 100.

merely trying to remove all evil thoughts and self-desires in order to release a person from the cycle of reincarnation.

Since the central teachings of Christianity contradict all other religions, it seems reasonable to first determine whether or not Christianity is actually true. After all, if Christianity is false then it would seem wise to seek out the truthfulness of other religions. However, if Christianity is true then it provides a grid by which all other religions can be evaluated. The uniqueness of Christianity demands that skeptics and seekers investigate its claims before they check out the claims of any other religions.

TIMELESS TRUTHS FOR A CULTURE THAT TEXTS

If no religion is the same and no religion is equally true, then the best approach to finding the truth is to start with the religious founder who is most unique—Jesus wins the contest hands down!

Question 3
Why Does the World Need to be Saved?

On June 28, 2005, Marcus Luttrell and SEAL Team 10 were assigned to a mission to kill or capture Ahmad Shah, a high-ranking Taliban leader responsible for killings in eastern Afghanistan and the Hindu-Kush mountains. After being detected by a group of goat herders, the SEALs were engaged in an intense gun battle. In the ensuing battle, all of the SEAL team members were killed except Luttrell. Although he was badly wounded he managed to walk and crawl seven miles to evade capture.

He was given shelter by an Afghan villager, Mohammad Gulab, who saved him from almost certain death at the hands of the Taliban. The villager and his tribe invoked a centuries old tradition called the 'Pashtunwali Code', meaning that hospitality, asylum, mercy and shelter must be provided for all who require it, despite their background and intentions. This village sacrificed themselves for Marcus Luttrell. In the truest sense of the word—they saved him. Although they didn't know him and he had done nothing to deserve it—this village chose to save him.

God did the same thing for every inhabitant of this world. God saw that everyone was flawed by sin and incapable of being in His presence. Jesus sacrificed Himself for people. He loved us so much that He did the unthinkable—He saved us. The only condition is that we must accept God's help to save us. Anyone can be saved—no exceptions.

One of the great challenges facing the modern church is how we should respond to our unchurched friends when they ask "Why do I need to be saved?" or "Saved from what?" Here are some reasons that demonstrate how we can better explain why a person must be saved:

REASON #1: EVERYONE FALLS SHORT OF GOD'S PERFECT STANDARD

All of humanity has failed to meet the standard of an absolutely holy and perfect God (Romans 3:23). We live in a world guided by moral principles where certain things are right and certain things are wrong. Since our world was brought into existence by a moral lawgiver, people must atone for the relational and moral gap that exists between flawed people and an infinitely perfect God.

Most people compare the level of their sinfulness with the sins of other people and feel that they will be able to make a "passing grade." However, it's important to remember that in a world orchestrated by the most perfect being in the world, everyone has an impossible hill to climb. God is infinitely greater in His goodness, holiness, kindness, and justice than anyone. Unfortunately, people are sinners by nature and by choice. This is the universal flaw of every human being—everyone has been touched by the evil effects of sin. McGrath makes a helpful observation in communicating the concept of sin to our friends:

> A helpful distinction which you can make when explaining Christianity to your friends is between sin and sins. Sin is like a disease, whose symptoms are sins. In other words, sin is what is wrong with human nature, and sins are the effects of this problem. Christianity is primarily concerned with sin—with the basic problem of human nature.[8]

God can't bend his perfect standards or He would cease to be Himself. He simply cannot stop being who He is in His very essence (I John 1:5). I like to pose the question this way: "How are imperfect people going to live in a perfect place with a perfect person?" This simple, yet powerful question can be very useful for people to think about the implications of living in a universe created by a moral creator.

REASON #2: DOING GOOD ISN'T ENOUGH

When people on the street are asked if they are going to heaven, most people reply, "Yes, I'm good enough!" In fact, the answer of the major religions is that we atone for our sins by doing good things or being a better person. However, imagine a scenario in which you were caught running a red light and caused a major traffic accident. You come before a judge in his courtroom to wait for possible penalties. Wouldn't it be

---

[8] Alister E. McGrath, *Explaining Your Faith*, 94.

absurd if you simply promised the judge to only go through green lights in the future? No judge would agree to this sentence. This would never pay the debt for breaking the law. Having broken the law, God justly judges us. We must make amends or atone for what we did wrong. Whatever our plan for atonement, it must satisfy the perfect standard of God. Sound impossible? That's because it is.

REASON #3: SIN NEGATIVELY IMPACTS OUR RELATIONSHIP WITH GOD

From the very beginning of human history, every single person has shown an inherent desire to do it their own way, to defy God's will, to ignore, or to totally forget about God. We resist the overtures of God to direct our lives. We want to make our own decisions and determine the direction for our lives. We don't want God to be in control of our lives. Unfortunately, there is always a relational cost to sin. Allow me to illustrate with the following story. Imagine that you steal your best friend's car. You feel guilty because of what you did but you have no intention of returning the car. Even if you walk people across the street, attend church, or treat all the rest of your friends with incredible respect—you could never have a meaningful relationship with your best friend. You would struggle to look him in the eye. You would not be comfortable in his presence. Ultimately, you'd have to resolve things with your best friend. No matter what you do, you can't ignore the car you stole! The sins we've committed against the moral creator of the universe has damaged our relationship with Him. In fact, the rejection of Christ, being a rejection of God Himself, is a sin of infinite gravity.

In addition to explaining why a person must be saved, it's important for the Christian to explain the necessity of Christ dying on the cross for the sins of humanity.

THE CROSS EXPLAINS GOD'S PLAN TO DEAL WITH SIN

Many people have a deep sense of guilt and personal inadequacy for decisions and choices they have made, as well as for relationships they have entered into throughout their lives. However, the Bible teaches that people can't atone for their sin by themselves (Romans 3:10). Because God can't ignore sin, Christ endured the cross for our benefit, bearing the full penalty that a morally perfect God must exact upon sin (Romans

5:8). God has no choice. He simply can't wink at sin or wish it away. Therefore, He showed His resolve by sending His Son to bear the full cost.

When we offend an eternal God who is absolutely holy and perfect, the debt that is incurred remains eternal until paid. How do you pay an eternal debt? Someone must help us. A substitute is needed since we cannot pay an infinite debt. This is exactly what Jesus Christ has provided for all of humanity. He was uniquely qualified, as both God and perfect man to pay such a debt.

THE CROSS EXPLAINS THE MAGNITUDE OF GOD'S LOVE FOR PEOPLE

God is the Creator of the universe and recognizes that all of humanity is morally flawed and incapable of having a genuine relationship with Him. Imagine the depth of love that God exhibited by sending Jesus Christ to Earth in order to restore that relationship. We actually mean something to God. The God of the universe did all of this because He deeply loves people—all people.

Of course, the Bible teaches that people need to respond to God's offer of salvation if we are going to benefit from Christ's death on the cross. If someone offers you a gift it can only be yours if you reach out and take the gift. What happens if God offers us forgiveness, yet we refuse to accept it? The remedy of the cross of Christ is similar to that for taking a drug that might cure an illness. You might recognize its potential but can't benefit from it unless you take it. The cross of Christ—as wonderful as it is—will not benefit a person unless they receive it (John 1:12; 3:16).

TIMELESS TRUTHS FOR A CULTURE THAT TEXTS

All the major religions believe that we atone for our sins by acting better or being a better person. Only Christianity claims that Jesus Himself (God/man) can pay our debt.

Jesus Christ

From the first century to today, Christians have called themselves followers of Jesus Christ. We believe that the character, claims, and miracles of Jesus of Nazareth separate Him from any other religious figure. No other religious leader claimed to be God in the flesh. No one else was crucified to atone for the sins of humanity before a morally perfect God. No other head of a religion rose from the dead to prove His claims. Jesus of Nazareth is truly unique in the pantheon of religious leaders.

To the surprise of Christians, there are many skeptics who take direct aim at the claims and acts of Jesus. For the person who has been raised within the church this can be a shocking revelation. Although the claims of skeptics may not lessen the love of a devoted Christian, it can hinder the faith of some believers. The journey of these Christians can take a dangerous turn when they inwardly doubt their beliefs or stop sharing their faith.

Although some of these questions may seem surprising for the Christian within the church, there is a growing segment of our culture that is seriously asking them. It's absolutely necessary that we provide clear answers to ourselves while providing a reasonable answer for others.

Question 4
Did Jesus of Nazareth Really Exist?

Time Magazine, one of the most recognized magazines in America, ran a special issue in the late 90s in which they tried to evaluate which of the last 20 centuries had the most impact upon the world. Listen to their observation:

> The 15th century was pretty wild, with the Renaissance and Spanish Inquisition in full flower, Gutenberg building his printing press, Copernicus beginning to contemplate the solar system and Columbus spreading the culture of Europe to the Americas. And of course, there was the 1st century, which if only for the life and death of Jesus may have had the most impact of any.[9]

It is truly amazing that in the eyes of the editorial board of Time Magazine the solitary life of Jesus Christ elevated an entire century to the very top. Why would this reputable magazine rate the first century as the most significant in history when objectors were claiming that Jesus of Nazareth was a mythical character?

To be perfectly honest, their objection really isn't taken seriously by anyone who knows ancient history. Evidence from both the New Testament documents and Roman historians in the first century clearly point to the historic reality of Jesus of Nazareth. Although some might question whether the New Testament documents are biased, it's quite clear that Roman historians acknowledge the identity of Jesus. It is interesting that four Roman historians (Thallus, Pliny the Younger, Tacitus, and Suetonius) took the time to mention a relatively obscure Palestinian teacher and miracle worker in their writings. Here's what a person can learn from these historians about the historic reality of Jesus:

- Christ had been condemned to death by Pontius Pilate, procurator of Judea, during the reign of the Roman emperor Tiberius (Tacitus).

---

[9] Walter Isaacson, *American Sketches: Great Leaders, Creative Thinkers, and Heroes of a Hurricane* (New York: Simon & Schuster, 2009), 197.

- At the time of the crucifixion, there was some sort of supernatural darkness, which some explained in terms of a total eclipse of the sun (Thallus).
- By the time of Nero, Christ had attracted sufficient followers in Rome to make them a suitable scapegoat for the burning of Rome. These followers were named "Christians" after him (Tacitus).
- Chrestus was the founder of a distinctive sect within Judaism (Suetonius).
- In AD 111, Christians worshipped Jesus as if he were God, and abandoned the worship of the Roman emperor to do so (Pliny).[10]

The eyewitness accounts from the Gospels don't hesitate to describe the life of Jesus at the same time that respected Roman historians acknowledge the reality of Jesus as a historical figure. All of this evidence points clearly to the historic reality of Jesus of Nazareth—there is no doubt.

TIMELESS TRUTHS FOR A CULTURE THAT TEXTS

If Jesus of Nazareth really existed, His claims must at least be considered. After all, He's the defining person of human history.

---

[10] Alister E. McGrath, *Explaining Your Faith*, 49-50.

Question 5
Are Miracles Possible?

Imagine you receive a text message from an acquaintance that informs you that he just had breakfast with your best friend. You are shocked for one simple reason—your best friend had a heart attack a month ago and died. You attended his funeral and gave a testimonial of the impact of his life. Immediately, you wonder if your acquaintance mixed up the names, had a dream, or maybe he's struggling more with your friend's death than you could have imagined. However, what probably didn't cross your mind was that your friend came back to life. As much as you would want that to happen, people usually don't come back from the dead—it doesn't happen.

Over 200 years ago, David Hume, a Scottish scholar and atheist who was a contemporary of Benjamin Franklin, challenged the intellectual feasibility of miracles when he said:

> A miracle is a violation of the laws of nature; and as a firm and unalterable experience has established these laws, the proof against a miracle, from the very nature of the fact, is as entire as any argument from experience can possibly be imagined.[11]

For two centuries, this thinking has permeated our culture. It's not the exception; it's the rule. Most people outside the church are highly skeptical that miracles happen. After all, in a world brought into existence by evolution and random chance there is no God to intervene and cause a miracle. The Christian must, at the least, provide common sense responses to the concerns of our family and friends.

---

[11] David Hume, "Of Miracles" in *In Defense of Miracles: A Comprehensive Case for God's Action in History*, R. Douglas Geivett and Gary R. Habermas (Downers Grove: InterVarsity Press, 1997), 33.

OBJECTION #1: MIRACLES VIOLATE THE LAWS OF NATURE

Most people who don't believe in the existence of miracles believe they are simply not possible. There is no argument or convincing reasoning—they simply assume that modern sophisticated people can't believe in miracles. It starts by simply defining miracles as a violation of natural law and it ends by stating that natural law doesn't change. This isn't a solid argument. It's an attempt to define miracles out of existence. Skeptics must eventually come to grips with the actual evidence related to the central miracle taught in Scripture—the resurrection of Jesus Christ. However, Christians can't be too quick to disregard the skeptic's refusal to believe in miracles. C.S. Lewis described the weakness of this objection in this fashion:

> This perhaps helps to make a little clear what the laws of Nature really are. We are in the habit of talking as if they caused events to happen; but they have never caused any event at all. The laws of motion do not set billiard balls moving: they analyze the motion after something else has provided it. . . . If God creates a miraculous spermatozoon in the body of a virgin, it does not proceed to break any laws. The laws at once take it over. Nature is ready. Pregnancy follows, according to all the normal laws, and nine months later a child is born. . . . Miraculous wine will intoxicate, miraculous conception will lead to pregnancy, inspired books will suffer all the ordinary processes of textual corruption, miraculous bread will be digested. The divine art of miracle is not an art of suspending the pattern to which events conform but of feeding new events into that pattern.[12]

I would be the first to admit that I have never witnessed someone coming back from the dead. However, I also don't believe that nature is the sum total of all reality. God, who is a transcendent being, who stands outside of the universe, is clearly capable of stepping into nature in order to set into motion those things that are not normally expected.

---

[12] C.S. Lewis, *Miracles: A Preliminary Study*, 60-61.

OBJECTION #2: MIRACLES ARE IMPROBABLE

David Hume believed that there was simply not enough evidence to believe in miracles. Legendary Christian apologist, Dr. Norman Geisler challenged his objections this way:

- The amount of evidence is not the same as the weight of the evidence. Hume adds up all the natural deaths in the world against the very few alleged resurrections and rejects the latter. However, his rejection doesn't weigh the evidence regarding Jesus of Nazareth being raised from the dead. His viewpoint would seem to eliminate belief in any unusual or unique event from the past, to say nothing of miracles. Rational beliefs should not be determined by majority vote.

- Evidence from the past cannot determine the present. Hume encourages the modern thinker to always believe in advance that miracles will never occur. This assumes that if a miracle did occur—rare as it may be—one should still not believe in it. However, this seems to indicate that he is encouraging a person to always bring his invincible bias against miracles to any discussion.[13]

Christians agree that miracles aren't probable. However, some of the most extraordinary (miraculous) events in the history of our universe were clearly not probable. Mathematicians even tell us that there is no mathematical probability that the fine tuning of the universe could have occurred simply by chance. Oxford mathematician Roger Penrose has actually calculated the precision necessary to create a universe with the various constants necessary for sustaining intelligent life—1 in 10 (10 to the power of 123). He comes to conclusion that all of these fine-tuning factors happening by chance are mathematically impossible in part because the number exceeds the total number of atoms [10^{79}] believed to exist in the whole universe. Although the miracle of the universe coming into

---

[13] Norman L. Geisler, "Miracles & the Modern Mind" in *In Defense of Miracles: A Comprehensive Case for God's Action in History*, R. Douglas Geivett and Gary R. Habermas, 78-84.

existence was not probable it was clearly possible if a person considers the reality of an all-powerful Creator causing it to exist.

OBJECTION #3: MIRACLES ABANDON SCIENCE

There are certain questions that can't be answered by physical science. For example, science acknowledges the reality of the Big Bang of the universe but it struggles to explain the exact cause. Kreeft and Tacelli make this observation:

> A scientist who believes that God caused the universe to exist had not abandoned scientific method, but merely acknowledged its limits. . . . He simply acknowledged that empirical explanation has its limitations, and believed that, in this case, the true explanation transcended them.[14]

It's important to remember that many people embrace an anti-miraculous bias for the simple reason that they resist the notion of a divine creator. Of course, if people deny the existence of God, there is no need to even consider the possibility of miracles. Obviously, miracles don't happen all the time. However, in a world that shows evidence of a supernatural being we should anticipate that miracles might occur from time to time. After all, as an all-powerful being, God can accomplish anything that is within His power and consistent with His character.

TIMELESS TRUTHS FOR A CULTURE THAT TEXTS

Miracles are improbable but this doesn't make them impossible. Just because something happens once instead of all the time doesn't mean it is impossible. Just think the Big Bang!

---

[14] Peter Kreeft and Ronald K. Tacelli, *Handook of Christian Apologetics*, 113.

Question 6
What is the Evidence for the Resurrection of Jesus?

On June 6, 1944, about 100,000 American, British, and Canadian soldiers climbed out of the water at high tide and landed in German-occupied France. Hundreds were cut down before they even touched the sand; thousands more were wounded or killed crossing the beach. Each year as we pause to celebrate this heroic act, the memories of the fallen grow dimmer with each successive generation. Imagine the challenge of Christianity as we attempt to keep the memory of the crucifixion and resurrection of Jesus Christ alive for every generation. It's not easy, but it's essential because his heroic act 2000 years ago defines our faith.

Pinchas Lapide, who is a leading Orthodox Jewish scholar, correctly observes the importance of the resurrection of Jesus with these words, "Without the resurrection of Jesus, after Golgotha, there would not have been any Christianity".[15] He proceeds to argue that only the resurrection could explain the drastic change of the emotions of the disciples:

> When this scared, frightened band of the apostles which was just about to throw away everything in order to flee in despair to Galilee; when these peasants, shepherds and fishermen, who betrayed and denied their master and then failed him miserably, suddenly could be changed into a confident mission society, convinced of salvation and able to work with much more success after Easter than before Easter, then no vision or hallucination is sufficient to explain such a revolutionary transformation.[16]

The simple reality is that the disciples of Jesus were not only transformed from cowards into martyrs, they were asked to believe in something that was outrageous at the time. In the first century, the religious establishment was divided into two theological camps. The Sadducees didn't believe in the supernatural and held that there would

---

[15] Alister E. McGrath, *Explaining Your Faith*, 68.

[16] Alister E. McGrath, 68-69.

be no resurrection at the end of time. On the contrary, the Pharisees believed that there would be a general resurrection at the end of time. However, no one believed in the concept of someone being raised from the dead immediately after dying.

Although Jesus foretold His death and resurrection (Mark 8:31; 9:31-32), nothing could have prepared His disciples to expect His immediate resurrection from the dead. Something truly remarkable must have happened after the death of Jesus that compelled His followers to embrace a belief that was truly strange by the standards of the first century. McGrath describes it this way:

> What the Jews thought could only happen at the end of the world was recognized to have happened in human history, before the end of time, and to have been seen and witnessed to by many. This is a startlingly new belief, and its very novelty raised the question of where it came from. Why did the first Christians adopt this belief? The event of the resurrection of Jesus, it would seem, caused them to break with (not echo!) the traditional beliefs concerning the resurrection. . . . It is too easy to overlook how strange the Christian proclamation of the resurrection of Jesus seemed in the first century. The unthinkable appeared to have happened, and for that very reason demanded careful attention.[17]

Although the unthinkable happened, this is not simply an issue of faith without evidence. There is strong evidence that points to the reality of the resurrection. In fact, there is an overwhelming majority of historians—secular and religious—who agree on the reality of five facts surrounding the death and resurrection of Christ. Two of the greatest contemporary experts for the resurrection, Gary Habermas and Michael Licona, explain the significance of this approach:

> This approach considers only those data that are so strongly attested historically that they are granted by nearly every scholar who studies the subject, even the rather skeptical ones. . . . Most

---

[17] Alister E. McGrath, 67.

> facts we use meet two criteria: They are well evidenced and nearly every scholar accepts them. We present our case using the "lowest common denominator" of agreed-upon facts. This keeps attention on the central issue, instead of side-tracking into matters that are irrelevant. This way we can present a strong argument that is both supportable and compelling.[18]

FACT #1: JESUS DIED BY CRUCIFIXION

The first step in developing a case for the resurrection is to establish the basic fact that Jesus of Nazareth died as a result of his public crucifixion. New Testament, Roman, and Jewish historians all testify to the reality of Jesus' crucifixion. The Roman historian Tacitus and the Jewish historian Josephus both acknowledge the crucifixion of Jesus of Nazareth. In fact, one of the most famous critics of the reliability of the New Testament, John Dominic Crossan, the leader of the Jesus Seminar, refers to these two historians when he makes this remarkable admission related to the crucifixion:

> I take it absolutely for granted that Jesus was crucified under Pontius Pilate. Security about the fact of the Crucifixion derives not only from the unlikelihood that Christians would have invented it but also from the existence of two early and independent non-Christian witnesses to it, a Jewish one from 93-94 C.E. and a Roman one from the 110s or 120s C.E.[19]

FACT #2: JESUS' DISCIPLES BELIEVED HE ROSE AND APPEARED TO THEM

At first glance, someone might think this is a biased and unreliable comment. However, this is not the case. The disciples of Jesus truly believed that he physically rose from the dead and appeared to them (Matthew 28:1-10; 16-17; Luke 24). The book of 1 Corinthians (AD 55) is

---

[18] Gary R. Habermas and Michael R. Licona, *The Case for the Resurrection of Jesus*, 44.

[19] John Dominic Crossan, *The Historical Jesus: The Life of a Mediterranean Jewish Peasant* (New York: HarperCollins, 1993), 372.

one of the most historically reliable books in the New Testament. 1 Corinthians 15:3-8 lists an early church creed that records the eyewitness testimony to the post-crucifixion appearances of Jesus. Within three to five years after the crucifixion of Jesus, the church had already put their eyewitness accounts into writing. Dean John Rodgers of Trinity Episcopal School for Ministry comments, "This is the sort of data that historians of antiquity drool over."[20] Finally, many of the early apostolic fathers (Clement, Polycarp, Irenaeus, Tertullian), who succeeded the apostles, provided strong evidence in their writings that the apostles had seen Jesus in his post-crucified state

FACT #3: PAUL, THE PERSECUTOR OF THE FIRST CENTURY CHURCH, WAS SUDDENLY CHANGED

Until his conversion experience on the Damascus Road, Saul of Tarsus was arguably the most violent opponent to followers of Jesus of Nazareth. His notorious pre-Christian activities clearly indicated that he didn't believe any of the claims of Jesus. In fact, as an incredible intellectual and ardent zealot of the Jewish faith, it makes no sense whatsoever for Saul to switch sides in this epic first century showdown between the Jewish faith and followers of Jesus of Nazareth. However, after the appearance of a risen Christ, Paul became a new man (Acts 9; Acts 15). He embraced the reality of Christ's resurrection and became the primary spokesman for Christianity. He witnessed something so extraordinary that it caused him to change all of his core beliefs. Listen to the significance of this change:

> Paul's conversion was based on what he perceived to be a personal appearance of the risen Jesus. Today we might believe that Jesus rose from the dead based on secondary evidence, trusting Paul and the disciples who saw the risen Jesus. But for Paul, his experience came from primary evidence: the risen Jesus appeared directly to him. He did not merely believe based on the testimony of someone else.[21]

---

[20] Gary R. Habermas and Michael R. Licona, *53.*

[21] Ibid., 65.

FACT #4: JAMES, THE SKEPTICAL HALF-BROTHER OF JESUS, WAS SUDDENLY CHANGED

The story of James, the half-brother of Jesus is truly remarkable. It is a spiritual rags-to-riches story. Like many within his family, James was skeptical of the claims of Jesus of Nazareth (John 7:5; Mark 3:21). Despite his early skepticism, we are told by the early church creed (1 Corinthians 15:3-8) that after Jesus appeared to him he became a follower of Christ. After his conversion, James was so committed to Jesus that he became the leader of the church in Jerusalem and eventually became a martyr for his faith. What could possibly explain James' conversion from skepticism, his public devotion to Christ, and his willingness to become a martyr? Habermas and Licona once again explain the significance:

> With James, we have another case of a skeptic converting to Christianity based on what he perceived was a personal appearance by the risen Jesus. As with Paul, we must ask the question: What happened to cause James to have such a conviction? [22]

FACT #5: THE TOMB OF JESUS WAS FOUND EMPTY

The overwhelming majority of scholars attest to the historic reality of the empty tomb. This confidence is based upon three realities:

- Christianity would never have survived in first century Jerusalem with a body still in the tomb. This would have gone against everything that Jesus predicted (Matthew 16:21) and everything that Christianity claimed (1 Corinthians 15:12-19).
- The enemies of Christianity believed the tomb was empty. As a way to explain the empty tomb, early religious critics accused Jesus' disciples of stealing the body (Matthew 28:12-13). Clearly this would not have been necessary if a body was still in the tomb.
- Female followers of Jesus testified that His tomb was empty. This might not make sense in the modern world where a witness is

---

[22] Ibid., 68-69.

believed regardless of whether they are male or female. However, in the first century, both Roman and Jewish cultures discounted the testimony of women. In this climate, there would have been no reason for the Gospel authors to make up the story of the women. This would have hurt their case unless they were simply recounting what actually happened.

TIMELESS TRUTHS FOR A CULTURE THAT TEXTS

The overwhelming majority of scholars—secular and religious—believe five facts that provide evidence that Jesus Christ supernaturally rose from the dead.

Question 7
Are There Non-Miraculous Explanations for the Empty Tomb?

History is full of hoaxes. Hitler's diary, Piltdown Man, the missing pages from John Wilkes Booth's, the Lock Ness Monster photo, and the Alien Autopsy Film rank as some of the most successful hoaxes. In a world that denies the reality of God and the possibility of miracles (supernatural acts), skeptics and scholars ardently believe that the resurrection of Jesus Christ must be the ultimate example of either a tremendously successful hoax, a mistake in ancient history, or simply a legend crafted over years and years.

In the previous chapter, we provided evidence with five clear facts that both religious and secular historians agree demonstrate the reasonableness of the resurrection of Jesus. Obviously, for those who deny the capacity for God to intervene into the affairs of humanity, they must supply alternative explanations for the empty tomb. Although research into this issue has revealed well over forty different naturalistic explanations, this chapter will briefly focus on some of the more common ones.

JESUS NEVER REALLY DIED

Skeptics love to suggest some kind of conspiracy that might have involved the bribing of the soldiers to make sure Jesus didn't die or to simply make it appear that He did die. They also like to question how we can be certain that Jesus of Nazareth actually died. After all, all of this happened so long ago in a less sophisticated and simple time. Here are a handful of reasons why the theory that Jesus didn't really die can't be defended:

- Jesus could not have survived the crucifixion. Victims of this type of violence experienced the most brutal of conditions including trauma, loss of blood, and shock (John 19:1-2; 17-18; Mark 15:16-19).
- The Roman soldiers—who were trained executioners—did not need to break his legs because they had already determined that He was dead (John 19:32-33).

- A deeply injured Jesus could not have recuperated in time to convince the disciples He had risen from the dead.
- The soldiers pierced Jesus' side with a spear to ensure that he was dead. The spear entered through the rib cage and pierced the lung, the sack around the heart, and the heart itself, which released blood and pleural fluids (John 19:34).

THE DISCIPLES WENT TO THE WRONG TOMB

Critics speculate that the women and the disciples simply went to the wrong tomb. When they discovered that the tomb was empty they falsely believed that Jesus had risen from the dead. Here are a handful of reasons why the wrong tomb theory can't be defended:

- The burial of Jesus in the tomb of Joseph of Aramathea is one of the most historically reliable events in the resurrection story (John 19:38; Matthew 27:57-61; 1 Corinthians 15:3-8). The burial place of a very prestigious man within the Jewish community would have been known by many, including Joseph himself.
- The women had seen where Jesus was buried (Luke 23:55). It's not likely that the women would have gone to the wrong tomb after only a few days.
- The Roman and Jewish authorities could have easily disproved Christianity by merely going to the right tomb, exhuming the body, and publicly displaying it (Matthew 27:62-66).

THE DISCIPLES HALLUCINATED CHRIST'S POST-CRUCIFIXION APPEARANCES

Skeptics suggest that the disciples must have wanted for Jesus to come back from the dead so badly that they imagined it. Here are a handful of reasons why the hallucination theory can't be defended:

- The disciples had not anticipated Jesus coming back from the dead after His crucifixion (Matthew 24:1-11). Like many Jews of the first century, they believed in the general resurrection in the last day. If the disciples were to project hallucinations of Jesus, they would have projected him in Paradise, where the righteous dead went and awaited the resurrection at the end of the world.

- Hallucinations are not group experiences; they are individual experiences.
- Hallucinations can't explain the empty tomb nor can they explain the conversion of Jesus' skeptical brother James.

TIMELESS TRUTHS FOR A CULTURE THAT TEXTS

Although many skeptics don't want to believe the supernatural explanation for the empty tomb, the alternatives make little or no sense.

Question 8
Was the Incarnation Necessary?

I have a dear friend, Darlene, who is a committed follower of Jesus Christ. Darlene is a married, stay-at-home mother of two, and a former engineer. She has a sharp mind and analyzes everything—including her own faith. From the moment she placed her trust in Christ while in college, her life has been absolutely transformed. She has experienced a deep sense of meaning, forgiveness, and a powerful sense of peace in difficult situations. However, she has never been able to escape these lingering questions: "Why did God have to become a man in order to save people?" "If God is all-powerful, why did He choose this approach?" "Why should God demand that someone so great die such a horrific death on the cross?"

It shouldn't be a surprise that many people outside faith think the same way as Darlene. The idea of God becoming a man sounds like a mythical concept. The idea of God sending His son to die on the cross seems gruesome and unnecessary. Increasingly, our unchurched friends struggle with the core idea of the Christian faith that God sent His Son into the world.

Before we attempt to answer these questions it's necessary to clearly explain what is meant by the incarnation. The expression "incarnation" refers to the act during which the pre-existent Christ took to Himself human nature. In other words, while still fully God (Colossians 1:19), Christ became fully man through human birth by the virgin Mary (Isaiah 7:14; Matthew 1:21, 25). Conceived by the Holy Spirit, He was a perfect human being without the sin nature of Adam (Hebrews 4:15). This act in no way diminished His essential essence as God, nor did it require He become two people. He would always possess both human nature and divine nature in one Person. The Christian claim that Jesus was God in the flesh separates Christianity from all other religions. C.S. Lewis called the incarnation "the Grand Miracle." He wrote the following:

> The central miracle asserted by Christians is the Incarnation. . . . Every other miracle prepares for this, or exhibits this, or results from this. . . . It was the central event in the history of the Earth—the very thing that the whole story has been about.[23]

Since it is necessary that Christians have the ability to explain what this concept means and why it is important for our faith, the following is a more detailed breakdown of precisely what we mean by the Incarnation.

THE DEITY OF CHRIST

Theologians use the expression "The Deity of Christ" to describe how Jesus Christ possessed the essential nature of God. In other words, Jesus was fully God. One of the great theologians in the 20th century was B.B. Warfield who said this about the divine nature of Christ, "He is declared, in the most express manner possible, to be all that God is, to possess the whole fullness of attributes which make God God."

Scripture clearly teaches that Jesus was truly God in every respect (John 1:1; 8:58; 10:30; Philippians 2:6; Colossians 2:9). Jesus is recognized in His full deity by virtue of His names (God, Lord, Son of God), His attributes (eternal, omnipresent, omniscient, omnipotent, immutable), and His divine works (creator, sustainer, forgiver of sin, miracle worker). In addition, Jesus received worship (John 5:23; Matthew 21:16) knowing full-well that only God was to be worshipped (Deuteronomy 6:13; Matthew 4:10).

THE HUMANITY OF CHRIST

Scripture also reveals that Jesus was not only God; Jesus was a perfect man. The humanity of Christ was demonstrated by the fact that He had a true body of flesh and blood (Galatians 4:4; Romans 1:3), developed in the normal way (Luke 2:40,52), possessed the key characteristics of human nature (John 13:21; 19:30), and had the sinless qualities of a

---

[23] C.S. Lewis, *Miracles: A Preliminary Study* (New York: Macmillan Publishing Co, 1947), 112.

human being in that He was weary, hungry, thirsty, and was tempted (John 4:6; Matthew 4:2; John 19:28; Hebrews 4:15).

According to the Christian faith, Christ had to be fully God and a perfect man. To rob Christ's divine nature of a single attribute would destroy His deity. To rob Christ of a single human attribute would result in destruction of His true humanity. As a man, Christ could represent man and die as a man (Romans 5:10). As God, the death of Christ could have infinite value—enough to redeem the sins of the whole world (1 John 2:2). Both natures are necessary for redemption. There is no other option. A human must represent humanity just like a perfect/divine sacrifice is the only one acceptable to a perfect God (1 John 3:5).

THE TEMPTATION OF JESUS

The temptation of Jesus is very difficult for both the theologian to express and for the majority of Christians to understand. Although Jesus possessed a human nature, He was utterly and completely sinless. However, despite the fact that Jesus was sinless, He was still tempted like we face temptation. In fact, Christ was repeatedly "tempted" throughout His earthly ministry (Luke 4:13; Matthew 4:1-11). Although theologians agree that Jesus was sinless and that he faced temptation, they differ on whether or not He could have sinned. Theologians usually view this issue from two perspectives:

- Christ could not sin—Christ was not able to sin because we're told that it is impossible to tempt God. James 1:13 clearly says, "For God cannot be tempted by evil, nor does he tempt anyone." For sin to occur there must be an inner response to an outward temptation. Since Jesus did not possess a sin nature, there was nothing within Him to respond to the temptation (Hebrews 4:15).

- Christ would not sin—Christ was able not to sin. In other words, His godliness and commitment to God were so great that He had the personal strength to resist walking down the path of sin. If Jesus was to experience genuine temptation, then He had to have been able to sin.

Here are some thoughts that might help clarify this issue. In His sinless humanity, Christ was fully capable of genuine temptation. In his deity, Christ was not only sinless (2 Corinthians 5:21), but unable to be tempted (James 1:13). In other words, He had the ability to be tempted (human nature), but not the ability to succumb to it (divine nature). It might be helpful to imagine a professional archer who is trying to fire an arrow at a target. Behind the target is a four-inch block of wood followed by a four-inch block of solid steel. Imagine that the arrow represents a genuine temptation and the block of wood represents the human nature of Christ while the block of steel represents the divine nature of Christ. We can confidently say that the arrow could penetrate the wood (Christ's human nature), but the arrow would not be able to penetrate the steel (Christ's divine nature). In His humanity, Christ faced temptation yet was sinless. In His deity, Christ was not tempted to nor did He sin. Obviously, the Christian doesn't have the advantage of a divine nature. However, God has promised divine help in resisting the pull of temptations (1 Corinthians 10:13).

TIMELESS TRUTHS FOR A CULTURE THAT TEXTS

Christianity not only claims that God exists; it claims that He decided to personally visit our world as a man. Christ was like us in his humanity (without sin) and was like God in his deity (sinless)—the perfect solution to our problem of sin.

Intellectual Issues

Most of us realize that there are a multitude of issues and causes within our world that explain why people resist the realities of the Christian faith. Many of our family members and friends are very confused about the Christian faith. They misunderstand what our faith teaches. They believe a caricature of Christianity. Life has thrown a series of obstacles which makes it very difficult for them to believe in the God of the Bible. It's vital for us to understand that many people have huge obstacles in their lives that seem to block any genuine conversation about spiritual things. One of the more famous Christian apologists and debaters, Michael Green makes this observation:

> I think of one of the atheists I met who became one overnight through the death of the father whom he idolized. . . . I think of another celebrated atheist, with whom I was due to debate. During the dinner beforehand, it became evident that the cause of her atheism was a series of terrible experiences in a Catholic school as a youngster. Another was a survivor of Auschwitz. Another was brought up in a strongly anti-religious home, and had imbibed his parents' attitude uncritically. . . . We must be people-centered in our approach and discover, if possible, what lies behind the atheist front. It may of course be sheer reasoning, but I have found that rarely to

> be the case. Whatever the cause, we need to find it out before we can hope to deal with the person appropriately.[24]

In our day and age if we are going to explain Christianity, we must also be committed to defend Christianity. If we can't remove the obstacles to faith, we might never have the chance to explain the life-changing message of the gospel.

---

[24] Max Anders, What You Need to Know About Defending Your Faith in 12 Lessons (Nashville: Thomas Nelson, 1997), 144

Question 9
Does Evil & Suffering Disprove the Existence of God?

One of biggest critics of the Christian faith, Charles Templeton expressed what so many feel:

> A loving God could not possibly be the author of the horrors we have been describing—horrors that continue every day, have continued since time began, and will continue as long as life exists. It is an inconceivable tale of suffering and death, and because the tale is . . . . the history of the world—it is obvious that there cannot be a loving God.[25]

It's absolutely necessary that Christians have the ability to defend why they still believe in God despite all the incredible horror in the world. I've found that the easiest way to approach this issue is to provide a reasonable explanation for why our belief in the existence of an all-powerful and all-loving God is still consistent with a world full of evil and suffering. I've discovered that one of the most helpful approaches is what philosophers call the "free-will defense".

God has decided to create a world in which human beings were given the dignity of free will. In a world where God grants people the dignity of free will, some people will choose to do evil. Although we would like for everyone to choose good, to choose virtue—the simple reality is that we can't! Jesus clearly recognized free will when He interacted with people in His public ministry, as reflected in the following verse:

> O Jerusalem, Jerusalem, you who kill the prophets and stone those sent to you, how often I have longed to gather your children together, as a hen gathers her chicks under her wings, but you were not willing.
> Matthew 23:37

---

[25] Lee Strobel, *The Case for Faith: A Journalist Investigates the Toughest Objections of Christianity*, 29.

Jesus, the Son of God, actually longed for the citizens of Jerusalem to respond to His message—but that was something that even Jesus couldn't do. Jesus could not control their free will because the nation refused to turn to the Lord. If God grants people genuine freedom to choose as they like, then it is impossible for him to guarantee what their choices will be. God does not tamper with our free will. He doesn't play mind-tricks with us—He doesn't hypnotize us. He gives us the dignity of free choice. God can create free human beings, but can't cause or determine that they only do what is right.

Alvin Plantinga, Professor of Philosophy Emeritus at Notre Dame is widely regarded as the world's most important living Christian philosopher. He has so effectively defended the free-will defense that almost everyone in the philosophical community has agreed that the presence of evil cannot be used to logically disprove the existence of God. Listen to his observation:

> To create creatures capable of moral good, therefore, He must create creatures capable of moral evil; and He can't give these creatures the freedom to perform evil and at the same time prevent them from doing so...The fact that free creatures sometimes go wrong, however, counts neither against God's omnipotence nor against His goodness.[26]

As much as people like to claim that the presence of evil and suffering disproves the existence of God, one of the brightest philosophical minds in our country has convinced his colleagues (secular, atheistic, and Christian) that this is not a logical conclusion.

As I travel across the nation one of the things that I've found extremely helpful is to give Christians an easy-to-remember statement for those who openly question the existence of God because of the evil and suffering in our world. I encourage people to use the following words, "In

---

[26] Alvin C. Plantinga, *God, Freedom, and Evil* (Grand Rapids: Eerdmans Publishing, 1974), 30.

a world where God grants people the dignity of free will, some people will choose to do evil."

In addition to using the free-will defense to defend our belief in an all-powerful and all-loving God, I've found that it can also be helpful to recognize that the skeptics' insistence that there is evil and suffering in the world is actually a positive argument for the existence of God. After all, evil is the failure to meet a certain absolute moral standard (murder, rape, torture, and genocide). The presence of evil in the world affirms that there is a moral standard. If we are the by-products of purely natural forces (evolution), moral absolutes don't make sense. Moral absolutes make the most sense in a world brought into existence by its moral creator.

TIMELESS TRUTHS FOR A CULTURE THAT TEXTS

God does not tamper with our free will. He doesn't play mind tricks with us—He doesn't hypnotize us. He gives us the dignity of free choice. In a world where God grants people the dignity of free will, some people will choose to do evil.

Question 10
Why Doesn't God Stop Evil?

It's a horrible feeling to get a phone call in the middle of the night with the news that a good friend died of cancer. It's agonizing when someone informs you that their loved one was killed in a car accident. In those moments, people not only struggle with loss; they also struggle with their own faith in a God who seems unwilling or unable to stop evil/bad events from happening. Repeatedly, friends and members of my church have come to me in a moment of grief and asked a simple, yet profound question, "Why didn't God do something?"

In situations like this, there are no easy answers. In fact, I think Christians shouldn't try to give a specific answer for why God may allow something to happen. We can't give people an exact answer for why God allows a specific event to happen. In fact, we shouldn't try--we aren't smart enough! We can't look at the past, present, and future. We can't see how God may reconcile things in eternity. We can't look ahead and see how situations change the world or change people.

However, when our unchurched friends think about the issue of evil, they naturally begin to wonder why a powerful God can't simply stop it. They begin to ask the following questions:

- Why couldn't God create a world without evil?
- Why didn't He stop the murderer/rapist from violating innocent people?
- Why did He allow the terrorist to commit a horrific act?

If we are talking to someone who is genuinely interested in thinking through this question, I believe it is important to explain why God can't simply stop everything that is bad in the world. Here are several things that can be quite helpful.

First, God's power is constrained in certain logical ways. In other words, there are certain things that God can't do, but not because He is somehow overwhelmed by the immensity of the task. It's simply a logical impossibility. Think of the following examples:

- He can't make a round object square.
- He can't make a rock so big that he can't move it.
- He can't make 2 + 2 = 5.
- He can't act in a way that is inconsistent with His divine qualities.
- He can't prevent people with free will from doing evil.

Second, God can't remove moral evil without contradicting human free will and the entire world that hinges on people's free choice. One of the biggest causes of the pain and suffering that come into our world is also the source for most of the great satisfaction in our lives as humans. Think of the impossibility of any of the following situations:

- If God was to stop evil, would He prevent the initial thought from coming into a person's head or simply freeze a person before he or she could commit the act of evil?
- If God had to freeze someone, how long would the person be paralyzed? When would he or she snap out of it? Would the person remember what he or she had been thinking about or would God wipe away the person's memory?
- If God were to regularly intervene He couldn't keep it a secret. If God was to stop evil, isn't it possible that people would become even more empowered to attempt evil acts knowing that some divine force was going to reach down and attempt to stop it?

It's important to remember that although we question God for allowing evil and suffering, we would question God even more if He didn't allow us the freedom to choose and pursue those things that bring us happiness and joy. It's a difficult trade-off. Most people would not be willing to sacrifice our sense of choice if this meant that we would lose the unique attribute of being human—the dignity of free will. Dr. John Feinberg offers this assessment:

> Has God done something wrong in creating human beings? Not at all when we consider the great value man has and the great worth God places upon us. As an empirical fact, moral evil has happened as a concomitant of a world populated with human beings. Still, it is

> one of those good possible worlds God could have created. God is a good God; our world of non-glorified human beings demonstrates his goodness.[27]

Third, God created the world with an intentional distance between Himself and His creation. Our world has been created so that human beings would have a clear picture of the consequences of their actions. Free will doesn't mean a lot if God is always intervening with our actions. God has established the natural world to run in a certain rhythm. God envisioned that people would understand the implications, both good and bad, of their rational free choice.

Fourth, John Feinberg suggests that although there are a handful of ways that God might have been able to get rid of evil, none of these would be acceptable to the person living in the modern world:

- God could eliminate moral evil by doing away with mankind.
- God could eliminate all objects of desire.
- God could eliminate all human desires, since sin ultimately stems from desires.
- God could allow desires but never allow these desires to produce actions.
- God could remove any person willing to commit evil.
- God could remove any public expression of moral evil by stopping human bodily movement.[28]

There are a handful of very problematic implications in suggesting that God regularly intervene to stop various acts of moral evil. If God tried to eliminate moral evil in this way, it would drastically change life as we know it. How could we imagine a life with free choice if God was constantly interrupting it? Quite simply life would be chaotic. In addition, it's simply not reasonable to imagine how God could miraculously

---

[27] John S. Feinberg, *The Many Faces of Evil: Theological Systems and the Problems of Evil* (Wheaton: Crossway Books, 2004), 180.

[28] John S. Feinberg, *The Many Faces of Evil: Theological Systems and the Problems of Evil*, 174-177.

intervene into the affairs of people. How can you stop people from acting out their thoughts? How can you paralyze people in the midst of their actions? Finally, if God supernaturally removed evil after creating mankind as a free moral agent, many people might question the wisdom of God in creating the world as He did. In other words, if God gave people the dignity of free will, why wouldn't He simply allow this approach to play out?

TIMELESS TRUTHS FOR A CULTURE THAT TEXTS

In a world where God grants people the dignity of free will, some people choose to do evil. God can't undo this reality—it would be catastrophic in every imaginable way.

Question 11
Why Does God Allow Natural Disasters and Diseases?

Far too often, a watching world believes God is morally responsible for things like earthquakes, tornadoes, floods, personal tragedies, and diseases. Whether it was the 2005 earthquake in India and Pakistan that killed 80,000, or the tsunami that hit Sri Lanka, Thailand, and India killing approximately 240,000, many observers struggle with God's inaction in our fallen world. As one newsman, commenting on Hurricane Katrina, put it, "If this world is the product of intelligent design, then the designer has some explaining to do."

Jesus was once asked about a collapsed tower that killed eighteen men who were working (Luke 13:1-5). Apparently, this collapsed tower—most likely an aqueduct built by Romans who employed local Jews—was a tragedy that was widely talked about in the city of Jerusalem. In the aftermath of this tragedy, there was a fair share of finger pointing. The Zealots in the 1st century would have disapproved of Jewish workers helping the oppressive Roman Empire. You can easily imagine the judgmental statements like, "Those men deserved to die," or "They were victims of God's judgment."

Jesus answered the questions with these words, "Or those eighteen who died when the tower in Siloam fell on them—do you think they were more guilty than all the others living in Jerusalem? I tell you, no! But unless you repent, you too will all perish (Luke 13:4-5)." Jesus' answer pointed out a very simple truth. God didn't allow that tower to fall on those unsuspecting workers as a way to judge the guilty. Jesus was shocked that people would attempt to claim that they knew precisely what God's purposes were for this event. In fact, Jesus didn't provide an exact answer for this tragedy. He affirmed the reality that innocent people will suffer and that everyone must be prepared to face God once this life ends.

The Bible teaches that disasters do not separate the wicked from the righteous (Matthew 5:45). We have no right to think that these events divide the human race into two separate categories of those who deserve God's divine act of retribution and those who don't deserve it. Unfortunately, tragedies only separate people into two camps—the dead and the living. They don't separate the saved and the damned, the religious and irreligious, the deserving and the undeserving. Here are some helpful insights when thinking about natural disasters:

First, don't assume that God is using natural disasters as a divine reprimand. Many of the events caused by the interaction of forces within nature indiscriminately target people within a large circle. In fact, the Scriptures (Acts 14:17; Matthew 5:45) clearly teach that the acts of God within nature indiscriminately affect both the righteous and unrighteous alike. We get in trouble when we assume that there's always a direct cause-and-effect relationship between natural disasters and the disobedience of people or nations. Obviously, God has frequently used the forces of nature as a way to communicate to His people and to judge the world. God sent Noah's flood (Genesis 6:1-13), the plagues of Egypt (Exodus 6-11), the earthquake in the rebellion of the sons of Korah (Numbers16:1-5), and the storm that forced the sailors to throw Jonah overboard (Jonah 1:1-17). However, it's very important that we understand that God did this in the Old Testament during His dealings with the nation of Israel. He had the luxury of dealing with the Jewish nation directly because He was able to deal with them as a distinct group that lived within a specific geographical circle. God is no longer dealing with a distinct nation that can be restricted within a certain geographical area.

Second, disasters and tragedies are built into the very fabric of life in our world. We live in an incredible and unique world. There is an extraordinary combination of 200 fine-tuning parameters and features that are absolutely necessary for any intelligent life to be possible—without them life on earth would not exist. Although the fabric of our fallen world uniquely sustains humanity, this infrastructure produces natural evils and destroys life. You can't have one without the other. These are intertwined; there is no way to separate them! If you remove the infrastructure, life on earth would cease to exist. If God were to remove these natural evils He would also have to remove or substantially change the natural processes themselves.

These laws, built into the fabric of life, are the immediate cause of many tragedies or disasters (earthquake, tornado, and hurricane). Of course, the forces of nature make our existence on this planet possible. If God were to remove them, He would also have to remove many positive and essential benefits to our universe. This is the downside of living in our present, fallen world. Remember, there is a vast difference between the world God originally created and the one that erupts with earthquakes, mudslides, and floods. Something is out of joint and our world awaits God to ultimately make it right. We are living on a once perfect, but now flawed planet (Romans 8:20-22).

Third, disease is one of the great equalizers and one of the great heartbreaks of the modern world. Although we live in an affluent culture with incredible advances in science and in the medical fields, no one is immune to the ravages of disease. It doesn't matter if you have a lot of money or are very successful, anyone can be hit by a devastating disease. God created a world in which people with free choice could live and function normally. Every single day we experience the amazing complexity of the human body, which has the remarkable capacity to work well most of the time. However, the human body can experience genetic mutation, the spread of germs, or the long term effects of our environment. These realities can lead to the trauma of disease, cancer, deadly infections, and life-threatening physical challenges. It's important to consider that as our environment declines humanity may become more and more susceptible to genetic diseases or cancer. It's possible that the increase of childhood diseases, Alzheimer's, and many forms of cancer is a direct result of an increasingly caustic environment, the absorption of foods that are detrimental to our health, and the presence of chemicals in our world and in our food supply.

Fourth, God is not obligated to preserve life whenever He is able. Although God mourns and is saddened by the death of innocent people, death in and of itself is one of the natural consequences of living in a fallen and imperfect world. Death will visit every single one of us at some point in our existence here on earth (Hebrews 9:27; Ecclesiastes 3:1-2). God is not obligated to rush in and preserve life whenever He is able. If He did; none of us would ever die. He could keep the whole population of the world alive indefinitely. Death is the ultimate fate awaiting every single person. Natural disasters attract our attention because the fate of so many people is decided at one point and place in time. However, when people suggest that God should rush in and stop disasters from happening, they are actually asking God to keep the whole population alive indefinitely. He will do that, but not in this imperfect world—in heaven.

Finally, disasters and disease remind us of the uncertainty of life. These events shock us to the core of our humanity. They remind us that all of us are on a time-clock—none of us are guaranteed tomorrow. Each of us is only guaranteed today. Leo Tolstoy, the famous Russian novelist ended his short story, "Three Questions" this way: "Remember then: there is only one time that is important—Now! It is the most important time because it is the only time when we have any power."[29]

TIMELESS TRUTHS FOR A CULTURE THAT TEXTS

Although the very fabric of our fallen world uniquely sustains humanity, this infrastructure produces natural evils and destroys life. You can't have one without the other.

[29] Leo Tolstoy, *Stories for Young People: Leo Tolstoy* (New York: Sterling Publishing, 2005), 80.

Question 12
Is Jesus the Only Way to God?

In 1971, John Lennon wrote the best-selling single *Imagine*. Its lyrics have encouraged people from across the world to imagine a world at peace without the barriers of borders or the divisions of religion and nationality. This song has had such a defining impact upon the modern world that *Rolling Stone* ranked it number three in their list of the *500 Greatest Songs of All Time*. The following lyrics capture the heartbeat of our world:

> *Imagine there's not heaven*
> *It's easy if you try*
> *No hell below us*
> *Above us only sky*
> *Imagine all the people*
> *Living for today…*
>
> *Imagine there's no countries*
> *It isn't hard to do*
> *Nothing to kill or die for*
> *No religion too*
> *Imagine all the people*
> *Living life in peace…*[30]

In sharp contrast to this melodic masterpiece are the controversial words of Jesus of Nazareth when He claimed the following, "I am the way and the truth and the life. No one comes to the Father except through me (John 14:6)." Although people universally respect the life of Jesus, they react with volatility when they hear Jesus' statement. The exclusive claim of Christianity is viewed as politically incorrect and a verbal slap in the face of other religions and beliefs. Listen to the words of famous skeptic Charles Templeton who questions the fairness of Christianity this way:

---

[30] John Lennon, *Imagine*, http://www.lyricsmode.com/lyrics/j/john_lennon/imagine.html.

> Christians are a small minority in the world. Approximately four out of every five people on the face of the earth believe in gods other than the Christian God. The more than five billion people who live on earth revere or worship more than three hundred gods. If one includes the animist or tribal religions the number rises to more than three thousand. Are we to believe that only Christians are right? [31]

How can we help our unbelieving friends to seriously consider the reasonableness of the exclusive truth claims of Christianity? The following two insights lay a foundation for why it's important to answer this question:

INSIGHT #1: THE CLAIM THAT ALL RELIGIONS ARE THE SAME IS SIMPLY NOT ACCURATE

If we don't challenge this claim people will continue to mindlessly believe the statement that "all religions are the same" or "all religions are equally true." For example, Christianity and Islam represent over fifty percent of the world's population. Christians claim that Jesus died on the cross for the sins of mankind. Muslims claim that the event never happened. Each of these claims represents the core of their religion. Both of these religions can't be right. At least one of them is mistaken. Ravi Zacharias, who is a great intellectual and worldwide spokesman for Christianity, explains it this way:

> Only someone who doesn't understand the world religions would claim they basically teach the same thing. . . . In sum, Islam, Buddhism, Hinduism, and Christianity are not saying the same thing. They are distinct and mutually exclusive religious doctrines. They all cannot be true at the same time.[32]

---

[31] Lee Strobel, *The Case for Faith: A Journalist Investigates the Toughest Objections to Christianity*, 146-147.

[32] Lee Strobel, *The Case for Faith: A Journalist Investigates the Toughest Objections to Christianity*, 154.

INSIGHT #2: CHRISTIANITY IS NOT THE ONLY RELIGION THAT BELIEVES IT'S EXCLUSIVELY TRUE

Although skeptics love to criticize the Christian faith for its belief that it is the only way to God, other religions do the same thing:

- Muslims claim their religion is exclusively true—they believe that the great miracle of Islam is the Koran, which is only recognized and fully understood in Arabic.
- Buddhism was born when Buddha rejected the authority of the Vedas (Scriptures) and the caste system.
- Hinduism is uncompromising in its belief in karma, reincarnation, and the Vedas.
- Atheism rejects any viewpoint that believes in a god or gods, or the God of the Bible.
- Pluralism believes that all religions lead to God.

If religions are not the same and are not equally true, then we must judge or evaluate all religious claims in order to determine whether or not they make reasonable claims that can be verified by information around us. After all, who wants to spend their entire life following something that is clearly not consistent with the vast amount of information at our disposal—how tragic! We must be ready, in the course of any conversation, to show that Christianity is a better option. The following are five tests that can provide evidence to a family member or friend that the Christian faith is actually a better option for how a person looks at the world:

TEST #1: CHRISTIANITY OFFERS A BETTER EXPLANATION FOR THE CREATION OF THE UNIVERSE—If a worldview can't explain, or is inconsistent with the truth about the origin of the universe, then it fails as a worldview. For years philosophers and scientists believed the universe was eternal—until science proved that it began at a single point in time. Christianity affirms that the universe had a finite beginning and was brought into existence by an all-powerful supernatural being who stands outside the universe. Three scientific observations (Big Bang, Energy Death of the Universe, and Fine-Tuning of the Universe) confirm that Christianity is consistent with science as it relates to the beginning of the universe. If our universe came into existence and it didn't just pop into existence, then the better explanation is a divine creator!

TEST #2: CHRISTIANITY OFFERS A BETTER EXPLANATION FOR THE FINE-TUNING OF THE UNIVERSE—There are 200+ parameters that had to exist within very tight parameters in order for Earth to sustain intelligent life. If only one of them were not true, life as we know it would not exist! The odds of this happening by chance are so remote that mathematical and scientific experts agree that it is a mathematical impossibility. I think the better explanation is a divine designer!

TEST #3: CHRISTIANITY OFFERS A BETTER EXPLANATION FOR THE EXISTENCE OF MORAL ABSOLUTES—We live in a moral world where moral absolutes exist. Murder is wrong, rape is wrong, and torturing innocent people is wrong. If a religion or worldview can't adequately explain the presence/reality of moral absolutes or doesn't recognize absolute morality, then it fails as a worldview. Absolute morality can't just pop into existence when everything has been developed through a purely naturalistic explanation of evolution. I think the better explanation is a divine lawgiver!

TEST #4: CHRISTIANITY OFFERS A BETTER EXPLANATION FOR THE POST-CRUCIFIXION APPEARANCES OF JESUS CHRIST—Most all secular and religious experts actually agree on five key facts (Jesus died, Jesus' disciples believed that he rose and appeared to them, Paul was suddenly changed, Jesus' skeptical brother James was changed, and the tomb was empty). However, there is not one secular explanation for these five facts that can stand investigation and reasonable thinking—not one. I think the better explanation is a supernatural being who can perform miracles!

TEST #5: CHRISTIANITY OFFERS A BETTER EXPLANATION BECAUSE IT IS TOTALLY UNIQUE FROM ALL OTHER RELIGIONS—If all religions are not the same or true, then the person eager to determine the most reasonable religion must begin by investigating the most unique or distinct religion. Jesus Christ, the founder of Christianity, made extraordinary claims about His identity:

- He claimed to be the Son of God—literally God in the flesh who died on the cross for the sins of humanity (John 3:16; 8:58; 10:30).
- He claimed that people can't fix their sinfulness by their own efforts (John 5:14, 22).
- He fulfilled over 350 prophecies from the Old Testament.
- He was supernaturally raised from the dead and seen by over 500 people as proof of His claims (1 Corinthians 15:3-8).

Because of Christianity's unique quality, it is strategic to determine whether or not it is true or false. If Christianity is true, then all the other religions are necessarily false because Christianity contradicts all other faiths. If it is false, then the seeker of truth has narrowed down the process.

Far too often, the modern skeptic makes statements about religion that really don't stand under the weight of scrutiny. Our friends may say that all good people go to heaven or that God is just looking for people with sincere hearts. Unfortunately, people expect that just because they see the world a certain way, or wish that it would be a certain way, this then perfectly aligns with reality. Once again, Peter Kreeft challenges the underlying thinking:

> How do you know what God expects of us? Have you listened to God's revelation? Isn't it dangerous to assume without question or doubt that God must do exactly what you would do if you were God? Suppose sincerity were not enough; suppose truth was needed too. Is that unthinkable? In every other area of life we need truth. Is sincerity enough for a surgeon? An explorer? Don't we need accurate road maps of reality?[33]

TIMELESS TRUTHS FOR A CULTURE THAT TEXTS

If all religions are not the same, shouldn't we try to determine which one presents the most accurate picture of our world?

---

[33] Peter Kreeft, http://www.peterkreeft.com/topics-more/christianity-uniqueness.htm.

Question 13
What about Those Who Have Never Heard the Gospel?

America is a country where the concept of fair play runs deep throughout our history. How many times have you heard someone say "that's not fair"? It can be a talk show host complaining about politics, a professional athlete complaining about how the coach is treating him poorly, or a fellow employee citing the injustices of being overlooked for a promotion. Imagine the outrage when a person realizes that people who have never heard about Jesus won't be able to get to heaven.

One of the most foundational claims of Christianity is that salvation only comes through personal faith in the crucifixion of Jesus Christ, who died for the sins of humanity (John 14:6; Acts 4:12; 1 Timothy 2:5). However, how is a Christian supposed to answer the following questions? If knowledge and belief in Christ are necessary for salvation, how can a person be held responsible if he or she has never heard the gospel? If billions of people throughout the history of humanity never heard about Jesus, how is that fair? How can God judge people who have never been told about Jesus? These questions can best be answered by stressing the following concepts.

First, God doesn't judge people on the basis of information they don't possess (death and resurrection of Jesus). God judges them because they reject the information already in their possession. Scripture teaches that every person knows at least three things about God apart from any special revelation from Him. Everyone knows that God is powerful by virtue of creation (Romans 1:18-20), that God is moral by virtue of conscience (Romans 2:14), and that God is good by virtue of providence (Acts 14:16-17). Instead of responding positively to these clear truths, Romans 1:18-20 tells us that people intentionally hold down the truth much like a person holds down a spring so that it doesn't pop up. A person's lack of responsiveness to general revelation precludes a person from receiving further revelation.

Second, God honors the dignity of free will. As long as people are free, there is simply no guarantee that everybody in the world will choose to be saved. In other words, it is logically impossible for God to make someone freely do something against their will. God cannot force a person to respond to natural revelation (what they already know about God). Remember, everyone has knowledge of God. It is up to them whether or not they respond to it.

Third, it seems clear that salvation has always been and will always be the result of God's grace and received through faith alone. Obviously, the content and nature of faith was different in the Old Testament simply because they did not know directly about the sacrifice of Christ on the cross. The Apostle Paul uses Abraham as an example of someone who was given the righteousness of God purely by his belief. Paul writes, "What then shall we say that Abraham our father has found according to the flesh? For if Abraham was justified by works, he has something to boast about, but not before God. For what does the Scripture say? 'Abraham believed God, and it was accounted to him for righteousness' (Romans 4:1-3)." The author of Hebrews describes Abel as someone who seemed to have understood the idea behind the death of a substitute and because he placed his faith in God was regarded as righteous (Hebrews 11:4). Gifted theologian, Henry Clarence Theissen describes it this way:

> Finally the Savior himself appeared. By his death he made atonement for the sins of Old Testament believers as well as for those of New Testament believers (Romans 3:21-26). God now offers to every man salvation through Jesus Christ. Prior to this age the plan of salvation was, in many instances, but dimly apprehended; now the whole scheme is laid open to every man that will know it. All that is required of any man is to accept what God has provided in Christ.[34]

Fourth, God will pursue everyone with His love. God desires that everyone experience His love and salvation offered through Jesus Christ. In fact, God's will extends to every corner of the earth and will reach out in an attempt to embrace everyone. The Scriptures clearly paint a picture of a loving God who reaches out to all of humanity (1

---

[34] Henry Clarence Thiessen, revised by Vernon D. Doerksen, *Lectures in Systematic Theology* (Grand Rapids: Eerdmans, 1979), 204.

Timothy 2:4; 1 John 2:2). If a person genuinely and sincerely seeks after God, there will be some way that God reveals Himself. God is able to reach people in ways we don't expect. He can reveal Himself—and has done so—through visions, angelic messengers, and circumstances that we can't comprehend.

Finally, we take comfort in the comprehensive knowledge of God. God's knowledge includes His awareness of what His free creatures would do under any circumstance. This includes what an individual might have done if he or she had access to the news of the gospel. It seems reasonable to believe that God, in His omniscience, understood that those who had not heard the gospel message wouldn't have believed, even if they did hear (Acts 17:26-27). If God knew that a person would of his or her own free will respond to the news of the gospel, He would find a way to extend the reach of the gospel to that location (Acts 8:26-40). It's important to realize that God is too righteous to allow people to be damned simply because they happened to be born at the wrong time and place in history (Genesis 18:25).

TIMELESS TRUTHS FOR A CULTURE THAT TEXTS

God doesn't judge people on information they don't possess. That would be unfair. He judges them on the information they have already received and rejected.

Question 14
Why Did God Create a World with Free Will?

Minority Report was a 2002 science fiction thriller starring Tom Cruise. It takes place in Washington, D.C. in the year 2054. In this alternative world, a specialized police department, "PreCrime“, apprehends criminals based on foreknowledge provided by three psychics called "precogs". Throughout the movie the audience is forced to examine whether free will can exist if the future is set and known in advance. Naturally, movies like *Minority Report* compel us to contemplate whether some other kind of alternative world would have been better than a world filled with so much horrific and gratuitous evil.

Most people realize that in a world where God has granted people the dignity of free will, some are going to use that choice for evil. If God knew that people would choose to do evil, why didn't He simply choose another world? Norman Geisler, who is a tremendous evangelic scholar, poses the issue this way, "But herein lies the severest test of theism on the problem of moral evil. God freely chose to create a world He knew would turn against Him and would bring upon itself and others untold human misery and woe."[35] So, to further answer the question of why God granted free will to the people he created, we need to take a quick look at all the other possible worlds that God could have created—only then will we be able to appreciate the world that God did choose.

WORLD #1: NO WORLD

While participating in a last meal with his disciples Jesus uttered the following words regarding the betrayal of Judas, "It would have been better if Judas had never been born (Mark 14:21)." Isn't it possible to ask the same question as we look at the incredible evil, sin, and chaos that is in our world? Why didn't God simply choose not to create a world? There are a couple of things to consider: 1) we are not able to make a legitimate comparison between something that doesn't exist and

---

[35] Norman L. Geisler, *The Roots of Evil* (Grand Rapids: Zondervan Publishing House, 1978), 58.

something that does exist, and 2) if a person is going to make a valid comparison, he or she should compare a world that doesn't exist with the best of all possible worlds.

Christianity doesn't teach that our present world is the best of all worlds. Quite honestly, we acknowledge that due to the freedom of choice, our world is hopelessly broken and full of evil. However, in a world where God grants people the dignity of free will, our present evil world is simply the best path to the best of all possible worlds. If seen from this vantage point, then a person can see that the best of all possible worlds—life in the presence of an infinitely perfect being—is much better than not having a world at all.

WORLD #2: AMORAL WORLD

Some people suggest that a world comprised of robots that do not have the capacity to sin is a better alternative than our present world. However, I'm pretty sure that most people would not choose to give up their freedom of choice. Freedom of choice brings dignity and joy along with the ability to create options that not only benefit a person but can also enhance their relationship with God. Is a world of robots or a world of animals (the absence of morals) really superior to a world of humans? How is a world of robots or non-moral creatures even capable of saying they are morally better? Remember, an amoral world doesn't provide a path to a physically and morally perfect world. Only a world with free choice provides this option.

WORLD #3: WORLD OF SINLESS ROBOTS

If the Bible teaches that heaven will contain free people who will never sin, why couldn't it be possible for God to create people with free choice who didn't sin? Although a person might suggest this kind of world, it seems unlikely that such a world could exist. God can't program people's free will. He can't tamper with free will. He can't hypnotize people so they always use their free will for good. C.S. Lewis makes this observation:

> God created things which had free will. That means creatures which can go wrong or right. Some people think they can imagine a

> creature which was free but had no possibility of going wrong, but I can't. If a thing is free to be good it's also free to be bad. And free will is what has made evil possible. Why, then did God give them free will? Because free will, though it makes evil possible, is also the only thing that makes possible any love or goodness or joy worth having. A world of automata-of creatures that worked like machines-would hardly be worth creating.[36]

Of course, it's also important to recognize that Christians in heaven are not the equivalent of sinless robots. People still have free will in heaven. However, the free will of Christians in heaven will be empowered so that we will choose to obey God and not disobey. All of our experiences in this life, along with our new reality in heaven, will empower our free will to prefer obedience to God. In a strange way, an imperfect world actually allows virtue and goodness to be chosen and achieved both in this life and in heaven. Geisler puts it this way:

> A world where evil never occurred is morally inferior because it would never provide occasion for achievement of the highest virtues or the highest degree of other good. The highest goods are dependent on the preconditioning of evils. Where there is no tribulation, patience cannot be produced. Courage is possible only where fear of evil is a reality. If God created a world where evil never occurred, He couldn't produce the greatest good.[37]

WORLD #4: A WORLD WHERE ALL ARE SAVED

Although we would like to think that it is logically possible to have a world where all will be saved, it may not actually be achievable to accomplish this with free creatures. Simply put, there is no world where every single person will freely choose to love God. C.S. Lewis has made this observation, "There are only two kinds of people in the end: those

---

[36] C.S. Lewis, *The Case for Christianity* (New York: The Macmillan Company, 1943), 41-42.

[37] Norman L. Geisler, *The Roots of Evil*, 58.

who say to God, 'Thy will be done,' and those to whom God says, in the end, 'Thy will be done.' All that are in hell, chose it."[38]

Those were four alternative worlds that God could have chosen to create instead of this present world. I've tried to provide some evidence that none of these alternative worlds are actually feasible. When all is said and done, we are left with the belief that this present world is still the best possible path to obtain the best possible world (heaven). Choosing this pathway is God's guarantee that the greatest number of people will experience eternal happiness and joy.

TIMELESS TRUTHS FOR A CULTURE THAT TEXTS

Although our present world is deeply flawed and broken, it is the best path to the best of all possible worlds.

[38] C.S. Lewis, *The Great Divorce* (New York: Macmillan, 1946), 69.

Bible

Christians face an enormous challenge as we attempt to be faithful to our belief in the Word of God. Our spiritual journey is absolutely dependent on the belief that God has revealed Himself within the pages of the Bible. Everything we believe has its foundation in the revealed Word of God. The nature of God, the incarnation of Jesus, salvation by grace through faith, the death and resurrection of Christ, judgment, and the future life are all found within the pages of the Bible.

However, we live in a culture that has little or no regard for the veracity of the holy books of religion. People are highly skeptical of any alleged truth that is found within the pages of the Bible. How are we supposed to talk to skeptics who question the Bible? How can we provide a reasonable explanation for our belief in the truthfulness of the Holy Scriptures? Imagine the ramifications if God's revelation is not accurate. How are we supposed to convince people of the truth of our core beliefs when the very document we follow is in dispute?

Each of the questions in this section helps the follower of Jesus to better explain the reliability and trustworthiness of the Bible.

Question 15
How Can I Trust the Bible with All Its Errors?

Internationally recognized critic Bart Ehrman has been tremendously successful in tapping into the widespread skepticism regarding the trustworthiness of the Bible:

> I kept reverting to my basic question: how does it help us to say that the Bible is the inerrant word of God if in fact we don't have the words that God inerrantly inspired, but only the words copied by the scribes—sometimes correctly but sometimes (many times!) incorrectly? What good is it to say that the autographs (i.e., the originals) were inspired? We don't have the originals! We have only error-ridden copies, and the vast majority of these are centuries removed from the originals and different from them, evidently, in thousands of ways.[39]

The reaction of many good-hearted yet uninformed Christians is shock and horror. How can I trust the New Testament? Why are there so many mistakes? What happened after the apostles wrote the original documents? What good is inspiration if God did nothing to prevent wholesale errors from creeping into the text?

Unfortunately, the soundbites of the critics have an unfair advantage over the ordinary Christian. It's like an ordinary person traveling to Las Vegas to play poker against a professional. It's unfair. The odds are against the novice. The critic employs a seldom used term like "variation," attaches a huge number to it, and says you can't trust the Bible. If we are ever going to help ensure that the Christian's journey of faith doesn't get sidetracked and derailed, we must help them calmly interact with these claims.

First, when evaluating the claims by critics who question the accuracy of Scripture it's very important to realize that most of the variants

---

[39] Bart Ehrman, *Misquoting Jesus--The Story Behind Who Changed the Bible and Why* (San Francisco: HarperSanFrancisco, 2007), 7.

(differences between manuscripts of the New Testament) cited by Ehrman are simply not significant. Seventy to eighty percent of all the alleged differences are simple things like spelling errors and don't impact the meaning of the text in any way. Most of us take for granted the modern convenience of communication—photo-copying, computers, and spell checking on our phones. The ancient world didn't have that luxury and most of the errors would be equivalent to spell check errors.

When I attended Talbot Theological Seminary back in the 80s I bought my own personal copy of the Greek New Testament. This was an essential part of my two full years of training in the Greek language. As I read and studied my Greek New Testament, I noticed that it contained just over 1,400 of the most significant textual variants. That's not a lot considering the incredible claims of critics. Here are a handful of interesting observations about these 1,400 textual variants:

- Only two of these variants involve more than two verses in length (Mark 16:9-20 and John 7:53-8:11).
- About a dozen involve one to two verses.
- All the rest affect less than a verse, and usually just a handful of words.

The facts cited by critics are simply not as grim as they would like us to believe. These differences are manageable and don't hopelessly corrupt the message of the New Testament. Noted evangelical export on textual criticism, Craig Blomberg makes this observation, "All told, a typical English translation of the New Testament will include around 200-300 variants in its footnotes, averaging roughly one per chapter of the various books."[40]

Second, critics like Ehrman claim that there are anywhere from 200,000 to 400,000 variants or differences found in the various manuscripts of the Bible. At first glance, this seems to imply that the entire New Testament is hopelessly flawed and polluted by errors. However, it's

---

[40] Craig L. Blomberg, *Can We Still Believe the Bible?: An Evangelical Engagement with Contemporary Questions* (Grand Rapids: Brazos Press, 2014), 21.

important to realize that this vast number of differences is spread over the enormous number of 25,000 New Testament manuscripts. Craig Blomberg cites the implication this way:

> Suddenly the picture begins to look quite different. This is an average of only 16 variants per manuscript, and only 8 if the estimate of 200,000 variants is the more accurate one. Nor are the variants spread evenly across a given text; instead, they tend to cluster in places where some kind ambiguity has stimulated them. Paul Wegner estimates that only 6 percent of the New Testament and 10 percent of the Old Testament contain the vast majority of these clusters.[41]

Sometimes, Christians are so stunned by the facts shared by critics that we don't have an answer. It's vital to understand that one of the truly great strengths of the reliability of the New Testament—the fact that we have more manuscripts than for any other ancient document—gives the impression that these "errors" are fatal. This is wrong. A handful of variants per manuscript is incredibly insignificant.

Third, the fundamental critique of skeptics like Ehrman rests on the premise that the differences found in the various manuscripts of the New Testament have totally distorted the meaning of Jesus' words and the Christian faith. This is simply not true. Although critics stress the importance of the number of 200,000 to 400,000 variants, the differences we do find do not place the reliability of the New Testament in doubt. Actually, we have discovered that 97% to 99% of all the New Testament manuscripts are unquestionably accurate to the original. Blomberg summarizes it this way:

> It cannot be emphasized strongly enough that no orthodox doctrine or ethical practice of Christianity depends solely on any disputed wording. There are always undisputed passages one can consult that teach the same truths. Tellingly, in the appendix to the

[41] Craig L. Blomberg, *Can We Still Believe the Bible?: An Evangelical Engagement with Contemporary Questions*, 17.

> paperback edition of *Misquoting Jesus*, Ehrman himself concedes that 'essential Christian beliefs are not affected by textual variants in the manuscript tradition of the New Testament.'[42]

Unfortunately, critics and skeptics have created a series of talking points that create incredible doubt and uncertainty regarding the trustworthiness of the Bible. They create the impression that those who copied the manuscripts were unqualified. They also suggest that the gap between the originals and copies of the New Testament have introduced a staggering cluster of errors that have clouded the intended meaning. This is not the case. God ensured that the Holy Spirit watched over the process of the inspiration of Scripture (2 Peter 1:20-21; 2 Timothy 3:16). He also entrusted the copying of the Bible to those dedicated scribes and conscientious leaders of the church. It created an unbelievably reliable chain of witnesses that ensured that the Bible, the most significant book in the history of humanity, would be available to every generation.

TIMELESS TRUTHS FOR A CULTURE THAT TEXTS

The New Testament is not hopelessly flawed and polluted by errors. Not a single Christian doctrine or practice has been changed or questioned due to the differences between various manuscripts.

---

42 Ibid., 28.

Question 16
Was the New Testament Written by Eyewitnesses?

I have a good friend Rachel who is a religious skeptic. Although she was raised in the Catholic Church, she no longer practices her faith and consistently doubts most of the tenants held by the church. She's not a bad person. In fact, she is extraordinarily nice and considerate. She is dedicated to her family and is active in her community. Although she read my first book she didn't get too far because there were, in her opinion, too many references to the Bible. The simple truth is that she no longer believes that the Bible is inspired by God nor does it contain infallible truth for the modern world. In large part, her skepticism is due to the tremendous influence of the opinion shapers and power brokers of our secular culture who have questioned the reliability of the Bible for centuries. Textbooks, classes at the university, and documentaries all state the same talking points—the gospel accounts of the New Testament can't be trusted because they were written in the second century by people who were not eyewitnesses. They have created a climate in which people are convinced that the Bible is legendary.

Unfortunately, the church has not done an effective job of providing helpful and common sense clues that point to the reality that the New Testament accounts were indeed written by authors who were eyewitnesses to the ministry of Jesus Christ of Nazareth. This chapter will focus on five very clear evidences that point to eyewitness testimony.

First, why didn't the Acts of the Apostles (written by Luke, a first-rate historian) include one of the most significant historical events in first century Palestine—the destruction of the temple in Jerusalem? History clearly tells us that the Roman army led by Titus destroyed the temple in Jerusalem in AD 70. This would have been a tremendously significant event for two reasons—Jerusalem was a tremendously influential city and Jesus had predicted its destruction (Matthew 24:1-2). In a book that contains a tremendous amount of historical detail (Acts 7; 8:26-40; 12:1-2; 24:1-26:32) why not refer to the destruction of a truly great city that confirmed the prophetic powers of Jesus?

A clear explanation for the omission of such an important historical fact is that Dr. Luke wrote the Acts of the Apostles before the event happened. This isn't too difficult to understand because a person can sometimes tell the date when a newspaper was written based upon what is included or omitted. For example, if you looked at any newspaper in America 15 years ago you could easily tell whether it was written a day before or a day after September 11, 2001.

Second, years before the siege and destruction of Jerusalem the church witnessed the martyrdom of the Apostle James (brother of Jesus and recognized leader of the church in Jerusalem) in AD 62, the Apostle Paul in AD 64, and the martyrdom of the Apostle Peter in AD 65. Here's the significance of these observations. The Acts of the Apostles served as an ancient obituary for respected Christian leaders. Luke had previously mentioned the martyrdom of Stephen (Acts 7) and James the brother of John (Acts 12). Why wouldn't Luke mention the historic deaths of these great early church leaders? Much of Acts reports the missionary journeys of the Apostle Paul. Peter was easily one of the most famous of all the disciples. James, the half-brother of Jesus was the head of the church of Jerusalem. The simplest explanation for the absence of these tragic deaths is that the Acts of the Apostles was written before the martyrdom of Paul, Peter, and James—well before AD 70.

Third, the earliest letters of the Apostle Paul contain one of the most powerful, yet ignored evidences for the fact that the gospels were written by eyewitnesses. Allow me to explain. The book of First Corinthians is one of the most attested books within the New Testament. Both secular and religious experts universally agree that this book was written between AD 53 and AD 57. Furthermore, 1 Corinthians 15:3-8 contains a statement that many experts believe was an early church creed. This creed describes the accounts of eyewitnesses,

> [3]For what I received I passed on to you as of first importance: that Christ died for our sins according to the Scriptures, [4] that he was buried, that he was raised on the third day according to the Scriptures, [5] and that he appeared to Cephas, and then to the Twelve. [6] After that, he appeared to more than five hundred of the brothers and sisters at the same time, most of whom are still living, though some have fallen asleep. [7] Then he appeared to James, then

> to all the apostles, [8] and last of all he appeared to me also, as to one abnormally born.
> 1 Corinthians 15:3-8

In the ancient world a creed was a memorized statement that contained theological truth that could be passed from one generation to another. Gary Habermas, who is one of the leading experts on the resurrection of Christ, states the following evidence that 1 Corinthians 15:3-8 refers to a creed:

> Virtually all scholars agree that Paul recorded an ancient creed concerning Jesus' death and Resurrection. That this material is traditional and pre-Pauline is evident from the technical terms delivered and received, the parallelism and somewhat stylized content, the proper names of Cephas and James, the non-Pauline words, and the possibility of an Aramaic original.[43]

Apparently, after his conversion on the Damascus Road and after a period of time in isolation, the Apostle Paul sought out James, the brother of Jesus, and Peter (Galatians 1:18-19). The purpose of this visit was to receive a personal accounting of all the events about the life and ministry of Jesus. Habermas and Licona describe the timeline in the following fashion:

> Jesus' crucifixion has been dated at AD 30 by most scholars, who also date Paul's conversion to between 31 and 33. Paul went away for three years after his conversion, afterward visiting Peter and James in Jerusalem (Gal. 1:18-19). Many scholars believe Paul received the creed from Peter and James at this time.[44]

At this point, a mere three to five years after the resurrection of Jesus of Nazareth, Paul received this creed from the early church that clearly

---

[43] Gary R. Habermas and Antony Flew, *Did Jesus Rise from the Dead?* (San Francisco: Harper Row, 1987), 23.

[44] Gary R. Habermas and Michael R. Licona, *The Case for the Resurrection of Jesus* (Grand Rapids: Kregel, 2004), 260.

states that many were eyewitnesses to the death, burial, and resurrection of Jesus Christ. This is one of the strongest pieces of historical evidence that the gospels were written by actual eyewitness.

Finally, for well over a century an overwhelming number of liberal scholars and skeptics have claimed that the gospels and other New Testament letters were not written until AD 160. It was an open and shut case—every major university and every scholarly work was based upon these assumptions. Because of this dating, they were taught that these documents could not have been written by eye-witnesses. Fortunately, a very significant scrap of papyrus (P52) was discovered that contained three verses from the Gospel of John on one side of the manuscript and two verses on the other side (John 18:31-33; 37-38). Prominent historians and experts have dated this scrap of papyrus from AD 100 to 150. Some experts are convinced that it "goes back at least to the reign of Emperor Hadrian, which was AD 117-138, or even Emperor Trajan, which was AD 98-117."[45]

The existence of a copy of a portion of the New Testament (although just a partial scrap) provides tangible evidence that the gospels were written in the first century. We have evidence that at a very early date, a fragment of a copy of the Gospel of John had already made its way from modern-day Turkey to a community along the Nile River in Egypt. This concrete physical evidence refutes those who claimed for at least a hundred years that it was impossible that the gospel accounts were written by eyewitnesses.

TIMELESS TRUTHS FOR A CULTURE THAT TEXTS

Christians don't have to take the eyewitness accounts of the New Testament by blind faith. Historical evidence tells us that the authors of the New Testament personally witnessed what they wrote.

---

[45] Lee Strobel, *The Case for Christ: A Journalist's Personal Investigation of the Evidence for Jesus* (Grand Rapids: Zondervan, 1998), 80.

Question 17
Didn't the Church Hand Select the Books of the New Testament in the 4th Century?

We live in a world driven by conspiracies. Whether it is aliens, governmental cover-ups, fanciful movies and TV shows, everyone is intrigued by the prospects of "what if". The *Da Vinci Code* by Dan Brown provoked tremendous speculation concerning the Holy Grail legend and Mary Magdalene's role in the history of Christianity. Although the book has been consistently criticized for its historical and scientific inaccuracies, it still became a worldwide bestseller by selling 80 million copies as of 2009.

This fascination with conspiracy theories fuels the thinking of many of our friends, from inside and outside the church. These friends have serious doubts about any claim made in history—especially religious claim. One of their specific concerns is that the selection of the books of the New Testament may be the backdrop for another best seller conspiracy theory.

Critics make a devastating claim about the New Testament—a claim that is every bit as deadly as the question of the reliability of the manuscripts. Many scholars suggest that the books of the New Testament were hand selected by influential leaders within the fourth-century church. They claim that those in power had the ability to frame and influence the debate by determining which books of the New Testament were officially recognized and embraced by the church. Bart Ehrman expresses his opinion on what happened to those books that were not accepted as part of the Bible:

> For the most part they were suppressed, forgotten, or destroyed—in one way or another lost, except insofar as they were mentioned by those who opposed them, who quoted them precisely in order to show how wrong they were.[46]

---

[46] Ibid., 44.

Of course, this has the potential to be devastating to one's spiritual journey if we are left wondering if "All Scripture is God-breathed (2 Timothy 3:16)" is really true. After all, what if the books in our Bible were hand selected nearly 300 years after they were written? How can we guarantee that the books that were selected were actually the books that were inspired by God? Since this is such an important topic it's necessary for the average Christian to recognize a handful of truths that are rarely talked about at church.

First, the early church recognized three universal tests that enabled them to determine whether or not a book was Scriptural. The three criteria were apostolicity, catholicity, and orthodoxy. These universal tests were the very standards that God used to ensure that no exclusively man-made book could somehow slip into the sacred category of being inspired by God. Each of these tests was precisely designed by the early church so that additional (non-inspired) books could not be added to the Scriptural canon.

Apostolicity refers to whether or not the books were written during the apostolic age. Put another way, the early church looked for books that were written by first-century eyewitnesses. Catholicity refers to whether or not believers from around the world were in agreement on the importance and use of these books. Orthodoxy refers to whether or not the books were faithful to the historic teaching of Jesus and the apostles. The twenty-seven books of the New Testament passed these three tests while other books failed. Remember, the one historical fact that is not in doubt is that the twenty-seven books of the New Testament are the only Christian writings that we can say with confidence were written in the first century.

Second, critics believe there was an incredible controversy and furor over which books should be included in the New Testament canon. In reality, there were very few books seriously considered to be included. Blomberg cites a study by Lee McDonald that details the thirty earliest known lists and catalogues of New Testament collections from the second through sixth centuries. He makes this observation:

> Exactly fourteen writings outside of the standard twenty-seven-book New Testament are commended at least once, though sometimes in separate categories that indicate the writer's or compiler's doubts about them. Ten of these fourteen documents appear on only one of the thirty lists.[47]

In other words, very few of these controversial books (Gospel of Thomas, etc.) were ever seriously considered as a genuine part of the New Testament. The idea that the church suppressed or excluded books from the canon is a myth created by critics to suggest that the church mishandled the process. Nothing could be further from the truth. The various lists of the New Testament canon were uniform in their inclusion of the twenty-seven books while routinely excluding other books. It's important to recognize that although some of the twenty-seven books were doubted because of their size or uncertainty regarding apostle authorship, other books like the Didache, the Epistle of Barnabas, The Shepherd of Hermas, the Preaching of Peter, and the Acts of Paul were always considered dubious.

Third, the testimony within Scripture clearly shows evidence that the process of recognizing the canon of the New Testament was already underway while the Apostles were still alive. Consider the following facts:

- In 1 Timothy 5:18, Paul quotes Deuteronomy 25:4 and Luke 10:7 as examples of Scripture. Since Paul wrote 1 Timothy in the mid-60s this would have been an extraordinarily short period for the early church to recognize books on a par with Scripture.
- In 2 Peter 3:15-16, Peter acknowledges that Paul's letters (Epistles) fell under the category of Scripture. This would have been a very short interval of time—between five and ten years.
- The early church fathers (Clement, Ignatius, and Polycarp) quoted and referenced many of the New Testament writings.

---

[47] Ibid., 56-57.

Finally, some critics believe that the Council of Nicaea in AD 325 was where the church decided which books should and should not be included within the New Testament. Blomberg correctly puts this false claim to rest:

> The Council of Nicaea in AD 325, convened by Constantine, had nothing to do with deciding which books belonged in a New Testament canon. Nicaea was all about formulating Trinitarian doctrine; the resulting Nicene Creed contained three articles about belief in the Father, Son, and Holy Spirit. Constantine did commission Eusebius to have fifty new Bibles copied and sent to key locations throughout the empire. Yet there is no record of any debate about which New Testament books to include; this very fact suggests that there was little or no debate among the church leaders present. Eusebius would have included all twenty-seven books, which he had divided into the categories of acknowledged and acknowledged with some doubt.[48]

Church leaders such as Athanasius (AD 367) reaffirmed that the canon should include the same twenty-seven books that are included in all of our English translations. In addition, further church councils such as the Council of Hippo (AD 393) and the Council of Carthage (AD 397) continued to ratify what the church had embraced from the late first century.

TIMELESS TRUTHS FOR A CULTURE THAT TEXTS

The church did not hand select the books of the New Testament. They simply affirmed what people had embraced from the first century of the church.

---

[48] Ibid., 67.

Creation & Science

On Christmas Eve, 1968, three American astronauts (Apollo 8) were the first human beings to go around the dark side of the moon and away from the earth. They saw something that human eyes had never witnessed—the earth rising over the horizon of the moon draped in a glorious mixture of white and blue. In the midst of this awe-inspiring experience they opened the pages of the book of Genesis and read for the world to hear, "In the beginning God created the heavens and the earth." It's wonderful that three great American heroes acknowledged what is becoming increasingly clear—the universe had a beginning that can best be explained by a supernatural being who exists apart from and not subject to the limitations of the universe.

Of course, many people outside of faith struggle with the Genesis account because it provides a supernatural explanation for the beginning of the world instead of a naturalistic explanation. However, beyond this philosophical objection, many people in our secular culture believe the Bible has already lost its credibility because so many concepts found within the first two chapters of Genesis seem difficult to comprehend in our modern world. The skeptic looks at the Bible and thinks, "If I can't believe the first two pages, how can I trust the rest?"

Christians struggle with the Genesis account for different reasons. Many Christians desperately want answers on whether their belief in the Scripture is consistent with the scientific evidence that surrounds our world. Other Christians are very concerned with compromising the trustworthiness of Scripture in an attempt to placate scientific evidence. Unfortunately, many of the issues found in Genesis have become very divisive within the walls of the church. They have become a litmus test for whether a Christian truly believes the Bible. Far too many Christians jump to the conclusion that only their view is the Biblical one.

My aim in writing this section is to address each of these issues for the unique perspective of the unchurched skeptic who looks at the origin of the world solely through the lens of science. Although I am firmly committed to the authority of Scripture, I simply try to explain these truths in a way which is consistent with clear scientific evidence. Although we may disagree on precise details on how God created the world, I hope we can always focus on those issues that are absolutely essential to the core of our faith—the primary issues of God, Jesus, sin, and salvation.

Question 18
Is the Concept of Adam and Eve Consistent with Scientific Discoveries?

Imagine sitting down at Starbucks and having a conversation in which you let slip that you believe in a literal Adam and Eve. I guarantee that an educated person or a committed agnostic would probably roll their eyes. In a world where evolution is one of the strongest givens in the educational/intellectual community, the very mention of Adam and Eve immediately creates a heightened sense of skepticism. After all, if we are the descendants of a long evolutionary line of creatures, Adam and Eve are just a religious myth.

Most people don't realize that the scientific evidence for the Biblical concept of an original Adam and Eve continues to mount. This chapter will provide a quick survey of some of the scientific evidences that support the basic concept expressed by the Biblical account of Adam and Eve.

First, molecular anthropologists study the origin of humanity by employing a variety of genetic techniques. Generally, what these professionals have discovered is that human beings display much less genetic diversity than any other species. Fazale Rana, who is the author of the ground-breaking book *Who Was Adam?* makes this observation:

> What do these finds indicate about humanity's natural history? Molecular anthropologists pose what they sometimes call the "Garden of Eden" hypothesis to explain the limited genetic diversity. This model maintains that humanity had a recent origin in a single location, and the original population size must have been quite small. From this one location, humanity expanded rapidly to occupy all the geographical regions of the planet.[49]

---

[49] Fazale Rana with Hugh Ross, *Who was Adam? A Creation Model Approach to the Origin of Man* (Colorado Springs: NavPress, 2005), 61.

Second, molecular anthropologists have also used something called mitochondrial DNA (mtDNA) as another method for tracking and studying the study of human origins. A 1980 study by biochemist Wesley Brown indicated that the origin of humanity occurred recently (about 180,000 years ago) from a small original population. In 1991, biochemist Allan C. Wilson used mtDNA samples that pointed to a recent origin of humanity (249,000 and 166,000 years ago) from one location and a small population of women. A Swiss and German team conducted one of the most exhaustive studies in 2000 and confirmed that the origin of humanity had a single location in Africa beginning 171,500 ±50,000 years ago. These studies are tremendously important because they describe with growing certainty that humanity had its origin from a single location and is traceable to a single female. It is reasonable to believe that these dates are consistent with the biblical record.

Finally, the Human Genome Project (HGP) has allowed researchers to glean significant information about the origin of mankind. A team of scientists from Perlegen Science (2001) discovered a similar limited genetic diversity among human populations. The findings from this group and others have all agreed that humanity had a relatively recent origin from a single location.

Reason to Believe is one of the most reputable Christian organizations that attempt to harmonize the Genesis creation account with all the available scientific evidence. Briefly, the RTB model outlines the scientific evidence for the following core beliefs:

- Humanity traces back to one woman (Eve) and one man (Adam).
- Humanity's early population size was relatively small.
- Humanity originated in a single location in or near the Middle East.
- Humanity's origin dates back to between10,000 and 100,000 years ago.
- God created humanity at the "just-right" time in Earth's history.[50]

---

[50] Fazale Rana with Hugh Ross, *Who was Adam? A Creation Model Approach to the Origin of Man,* 51-52.

Numerous studies provide strong evidence that humanity originated recently (around 100,000 years ago, plus or minus 20,000 years), at a single location (East Africa), and from a small group of individuals. The Biblical account of an original couple (Adam and Eve) in a single location is not only reasonable, it is highly likely.

TIMELESS TRUTHS FOR A CULTURE THAT TEXTS

The story of Adam and Eve is not biblical fantasy—it's historical reality. Science can trace the roots of humanity back to one woman who lived in a single location from between 10,000 and 100,000 years ago.

Question 19

Is the Order of the Creation Days (Genesis 1) Consistent with Scientific Truth?

Steve Allen, America's dean of intelligent comedy doesn't think the Bible is a laughing matter. In fact, he makes the following assessment regarding the reliability of the Bible in the face of science:

> It is now recognized by every intelligent and informed person that the two {Genesis and science} cannot be reconciled. . . . Nor should we be guilty of the error of assuming that the problem relates only to Genesis. It touches the New Testament as well.[51]

Unfortunately, this perception is rampant throughout our secular culture. Far too many people no longer consider the creation of the world by God as a remote possibility. What is a Christian supposed to say when a growing segment of the population asks a simple question, "why believe the Bible when the first pages are wrong?" Think about it. When intelligent atheists and scientists insist through books and public speaking that the first chapters of the Bible are full of inaccuracies it's easier to understand why your average non-Christian may doubt the accuracy of the Bible.

The order of the creation days provides two primary difficulties for Christians who don't just embrace something at face value but want solid answers for what they read. First, many skeptics struggle with the Genesis creation account because the description and order of the six days of creation are difficult to explain in light of modern science. For example, some question how the lights became present on Day Four although we are told that God commanded the light to exist in Day One? Second, many Christians struggle with traditional explanations of these creation days because those explanations are based upon the assumption of a young earth or six-literal creation days.

---

[51] Steve Allen in Hugh Ross, *A Matter of Days*, (Colorado Springs, NavPress, 2004),17.

Interpreting Genesis 1, while using the corroboration of modern science, actually provides a compelling example of the truthfulness of the Genesis account. It's important to realize that Genesis 1 provides a description of the various creation events from the unique perspective of an earth-bound observer. In other words, the author of Genesis was simply describing the transformation of the planet as if he was watching it unfold from vantage point of the surface of the earth. The description in Genesis attempts to describe how God transforms a planet that is formless and void (Genesis 1:1-2) into a place in which mankind (Genesis 1:26-28) could survive.

Day 1 (Genesis 1:3-5): Light appears through the opaque atmosphere that would have covered the earth. In other words, light penetrated Earth's dark shroud for the first time. The day-night cycle would have become detectable on the surface of the earth. With the earth now exposed to light, photosynthesis could begin the process of laying a foundation for a complex ecosystem.

Day 2 (Genesis 1:6-8): The water cycle begins when God starts the formation of the troposphere, which is the layer of our atmosphere where clouds and humidity benefit our Earth. Water is now available in a perfect balance to set the stage for the next step in the formation of Earth into a habitable environment.

Day 3 (Genesis 1:9-13): Dry land appears for the very first time on Earth. Although solid ground had already existed it was under water until this point in time. Remember, Genesis 1:2 told us that the "Spirit of God was over the surface of the water." In other words, until this moment the surface of the earth was completely covered by water. What's interesting is that geologists tell us "that over a period of 4.56 billion years, Earth's land mass grew from 0 percent to 29 percent of the planetary surface."[52]

Day 4 (Genesis 1:14-19): This day was one of the most significant in terms of what an earth-bound observer might have seen. For the first

---

[52] Huge Ross, *Navigating Genesis: A Scientist's Journey Through Genesis 1-11* (Covina: Reasons to Believe, 2014), 48.

time, the Sun, Moon, and stars became distinctly visible from the perspective of the Earth's surface. This was significant because for the first time these celestial lights served as clear indicators of day and night and the various seasons during a year.

Some skeptics struggle with the implications of day four because they question the scientific feasibility of God waiting until day four to create the Sun and the Moon. It's important to remember that God had already created the Sun and the stars before the first creation day of earth. Genesis 1:16-17 could easily have been a brief review of what the Creator had already accomplished. The author felt compelled to remind the reader of what had already happened because for the first time in day four these lights are permanently visible from the surface of the earth. Hugh Ross describes it this way:

> The echo of wording from day one (verse 3-5) is significant. It suggests both when and why God created the heavenly lights. The mention of . . . heavens and earth in Genesis 1:1 places the existence of the Sun and stars before the first creation day; thus, the Sun was already in place to fulfill its role on the first creation day.[53]

Day 5 (Genesis 1:20-23): Day five recognizes the introduction of small or minute creatures in both the water and the air. Ross describes the significance of the Hebrew terms this way, "Scientifically speaking, when used for land life, it usually includes amphibians, reptiles, and insects. When used for fresh or saltwater creatures, it typically includes mollusks, crustaceans, fish, and amphibians."[54]

Genesis 1:20-21 also introduces animal species that are different than those previously mentioned. These species of animals are soulish creatures. In other words, they have emotions and will and are aware of their surroundings. Of course, they are not made in God's image because the author is waiting for day six to reveal the crowning jewels of God's creative activity. However, the creatures made on day five are

---

53 Hugh Ross, 54.

54 Ibid., 57.

described by the Hebrew word *nepesh*, which "denotes any species characterized by what scientists would identify as a nurturing behavior toward progeny or mate or both." [55] Ross further describes the uniqueness of these creatures this way:

> Unlike other animals, *nepesh* creatures can be trained to perform tasks that are irrelevant to their survival. They respond to human authority and personality. They show delight, sadness, fear, anger, and more. They form emotional bonds with humans. Obviously, though, some *nepesh* are much more capable than others to bond with humans and to serve and please humans.[56]

Day 6 (Genesis 1:24-31): Day six focuses on three specific kinds of land animals: "livestock, creatures that move along the ground, and wild animals." Each of these categories of animals is mentioned because it sets the stage for God's explanation of his crowning achievement in the six days of creation—humanity. All of the previous days of creation were necessary for humanity to successfully inhabit the planet.

The six days of the creation account were designed to explain God's ultimate purpose in creating the world so that beings made in His image could respond to His love. These six days are consistent with the best scientific evidence of how Earth came into being. Fortunately, the six days of Genesis tell us not merely how our world was created—it tells us why.

TIMELESS TRUTHS FOR A CULTURE THAT TEXTS

The six days of God's creative activity as recorded in Genesis do not provide evidence that the Bible is unscientific. It shows that they are compatible.

---

[55] Ibid., 60.

[56] Ibid., 60.

Question 20
How Old is the Universe? Does it Matter?

Most Christians agree that God brought the universe into existence. They look at the Genesis account as clear evidence that there was a supernatural cause behind our world. A year ago, I was speaking at a church on the topic of *How to Disarm Your Doubts*. The sole purpose was to provide people the tools to get the upper hand on the powerful doubts that wreak havoc in one's life. At the conclusion of my talk, I was approached by a middle-aged man who was eager to get my opinion on one topic—do I believe in a young earth or old earth? He was very passionate and insistent on knowing my opinion on this issue.

As we began to have a conversation I sensed that he was intent on dismissing or accepting everything I said based upon my answer to this one question. I wasn't upset by this nor was I mad at him. I knew for certain that this delightful man was a Christian and not a skeptic. Here's why I mention my encounter with this dedicated follower of Jesus. The debate over the old/young earth is simply not a relevant question for secular skeptics and intellectuals. The abundance of scientific evidence points to the age of the universe as being from 12 billion to 20 billion years old. The idea that the beginning of the universe and earth dates from 6,000 to 10,000 years is very difficult for people outside the faith to believe.

With this in mind, I believe that appealing to the evidence for an old universe, along with the Biblical evidence for a divine creator, is the most effective approach for our unchurched friends. The most effective way to gain a foothold with our unchurched friends is to provide clear evidence that the universe had a beginning. Ultimately, the skeptic must wrestle with a single question, "Which world view (naturalistic or divine designer) best explains the beginning of the universe?"

The book of Genesis begins its description of the universe this way, "1In the beginning God created the heavens and the earth. 2Now the earth was formless and empty, darkness was over the surface of the deep, and the Spirit of God was hovering over the waters (Genesis 1:1-2)." I believe verse one explains God's initial handiwork in creating the universe while verse two simply begins to describe the long process in which God made our planet habitable for the crowning jewel of creation—humanity. In other words, it explains how our planet becomes suitable for hosting humanity.

This approach to the Genesis account seems to be the most consistent with the overwhelming evidence of science that believes that the universe had a finite beginning rather than the infinite past of prior naturalistic and philosophical scenarios. Although entire books have been written on this subject, I would like to quickly suggest six different reasons why I believe it is more reasonable to believe in an old universe/earth.

First, astronomical study (COBE, 1992) has clearly provided evidence for the beginning of the universe through the Big Bang. Allan R. Sandage, who spent his life measuring the universe and became the most influential astronomer of his generation, "estimated a universe 20 billion years old."[57] Christian scientists like Hugh Ross describe the implications this way, "This extraordinarily low and smooth temperature in the cosmic background radiation convinced astronomers that the universe must have had an extremely hot beginning about 15 to 20 billion years ago."[58]

If the universe had a beginning rather than always existing, then we have to determine whether it is more reasonable that the universe happened by chance or whether it was created at a finite point in time by an all-powerful, transcendent being. Mathematical experts suggest it is impossible for the universe, with over 200+ fine-tuning parameters to have occurred merely by chance. The belief that the universe began at a moment in time perfectly complements the truth that God created the universe.

---

[57] Larry Witham, *By Design: Science and the Search for God* (San Francisco: Encounter Books, 2003), 70.

[58] Hugh Ross, *The Creator and the Cosmos: How the Greatest Scientific Discoveries of the Century Reveal God* (Colorado Springs, NavPress, 1993), 22-23.

Second, most distant galaxies and quasars are ten billion light-years away which, on the surface indicates the universe is at least that old. Some young earth creationists try to sidestep this issue by claiming that the universe is much smaller so light would only need a few years to travel the distance. However, if the universe was as small as some suggest, then the stars and galaxies that we see in our telescopes would actually be too small for gravity to hold them together.

Third, proponents of the young earth model have tremendous difficulty explaining the geological record of our planet. To suggest that nearly all of the fossils were laid down during the one-year time period of the Flood stretches the imagination. The presence of fragile fossils or layered deposits provides evidence that the geological record was laid down over time and not solely due to a cataclysmic event.

Fourth, calculations of how stars are formed point to stars that are billions of years old. Although some claim that God created stars with the appearance of age, this implies that God was okay with His creative works providing an illusion of what the universe looks like rather than accurately declaring His glory (Psalm 19; Romans 1:18-20). The calculations of earth and lunar rocks using radioactive decay clearly point to the age of these two planets in the time span of billions of years rather than thousands of years.

Fifth, although the Bible never states the exact age of the universe, there seems to be some evidence that points to an older universe. Revelation predicts that at the end of the world there will be an earthquake worse than anything we've seen "since man has been on earth" (Revelation 16:18). This seems to imply that very significant earthquakes were present before humans were on the planet. Psalm 102:25-26 tells us that the heavens will "wear out like a garment," which seems to fit most consistently with a universe that is billions of years old rather than mere thousands of years.

Finally, the old universe model allows for a description of the Earth that is most consistent with the overwhelming scientific evidence that believes our planet is approximately 4.5 billion years old. Genesis 1:1-2 describes the beginning of the entire universe and how God fashioned our planet to be the perfect habitat for the crowning jewel of His creation—humanity. The description in verse two fits perfectly with how our planet may have started in its infancy:

- Earth would have begun as a totally uninhabitable place ("earth was formless and void").
- Earth's surface would have been completely covered by water ("Spirit of God was over the surface of the water").
- Earth would have been covered by an opaque atmosphere which would have prevented the sun from shining through ("darkness was over the earth").

Hugh Ross makes an observation which lends credence to this view of verses one and two:

> Water did, indeed, initially cover all of Earth's crust. The "formless" and "empty" conditions of Earth—relative to life—would appropriately depict a roiling surface shrouded in darkness by an opaque atmosphere and an accompanying cloud of interplanetary debris. Without light on Earth's surface, photosynthesis could not occur. With large pieces of interplanetary debris crashing onto Earth's surface at that time, no surface life could have survived. We can easily understand why we find no evidence of life on Earth prior to 3.8 billion years ago.[59]

Too many Christians believe that the Biblical evidence and the scientific evidence are at odds with each other. The Scripture contains truth because it was inspired by God and without error (2 Timothy 3:16). However, we can also glean truth about our world from evidence left in nature by its Creator (Psalm 19).

TIMELESS TRUTHS FOR A CULTURE THAT TEXTS

The Genesis account of the creation of the universe not only confirms the observation of the Bible—it stands the test of the best science of our day. It's a winning combination.

---

[59] Hugh Ross, *Navigating Genesis: A Scientist's Journey Through Genesis 1-11*, 36.

Question 21
Should the Genealogies in Genesis Be Used to Date the Origin of Humanity?

Ancestry.com is featured through many commercials on TV. It's the world's largest online family history resource with 16+ billion records. The appeal is obvious. Who wouldn't want to discover what makes you uniquely you. They even offer the customer the opportunity through AncestryDNA the chance to uncover your ethnic mix and distant relatives.

The genealogies of the Bible were designed to help people do the same thing. They were written with the simple intent of transmitting important information from generation to generation—many times it was so that we could trace the line of the Messiah down through the ages. However, many God-fearing and devout Christians use the genealogies within the book of Genesis to substantiate the belief that the earth is 6,000 to 10,000 years old rather than billions of years old. They believe that the genealogies in Genesis 5 and Genesis 11 provide a precise chronological timeline that reveals the date for Adam and Eve's creation. They are adamant that one's belief in the authority of the Scriptures mandates believing in a young earth—there are no other options.

With this mindset in view, I believe it's important for every Christian to take a fresh look at the purpose behind the biblical genealogies.

First, it is important to understand that the genealogies were never designed as a chronological timeline, but as a technique by which to communicate theological truths. In other words, the chronologies in Genesis and throughout the Bible were not written as exhaustive methods for measuring the passage of time. The authors were simply intent on transmitting important information from generation to generation.

Second, Moses, the writer of Genesis 5 and 11 regularly omitted and condensed the genealogies as a way to focus on the most important names. Remember, acknowledging the presence of gaps within the genealogies is not an admission that a person doesn't believe in the inerrancy of Scripture. The genealogies were simply written for a different purpose—to communicate a theological message and not to measure time. In fact, genealogies were organized in the Bible according to patterns that would assist the reader in memorizing the content. For example, the genealogy in Matthew 1 is organized in three sets of 14 names. [Note: Matthew's genealogy skips certain names found in 1 Chronicles 1-9]. Genesis 5 and 11 use two sets of 10 names as a pattern. Since the authors of the books of the Bible chose an approach designed to enhance the communication of valued information from one generation to another, they often dropped names from the lists.

Third, as a person reads a Biblical genealogy they will see the words "father" and "son." Although we typically understand the terms father and son in reference to one's immediate child, these words can refer to one's ancestor or a descendant. Likewise, the word "begot" is not limited to the immediate biological child. It can refer to the father being the parent of all his child's descendants.

Although we want to be cautious in our use of genealogies let's be sure that we don't minimize their significance. Biblical genealogies can provide helpful insights into the history of civilization. Genesis 10:25 states, "one was named Peleg, because in his time the earth was divided." Many scholars believe this refers to a time period in the history of our planet when the land bridge linking the Western and Eastern Hemispheres was broken. Dr. Ross makes the following conclusion:

> Radiocarbon dating places the breaking of the Bering Land Bridge at 11,000 years ago. . . . If life spans in the Genesis 11 genealogy are proportional to the passage of time (which may not be the case), then the dates for Abraham and Peleg place the Flood of Noah at roughly 20,000 to 30,000 years ago, and the creation of Adam and Eve would have been a few tens of thousands of years earlier.[60]

Biblical genealogies are an important part of Biblical revelation. They confirm the line of the Messiah, provide an overview of civilization, and

---

[60] Fazale Rana with Hugh Ross, *Who was Adam? A Creation Model Approach to the Origin of Man*, 47.

demonstrate the feasibility of the origin of humanity. We simply have to recognize the inherent limitations of genealogies because these important features of the Biblical record were written to convey information, not as an exact measurement of the passage of time.

TIMELESS TRUTHS FOR A CULTURE THAT TEXTS

Chronologies were not written to measure the exact passage of time. They were written to transmit important information from generation to generation.

Question 22
Are the Days Mentioned in the Genesis Account Literal 24-Hour Days?

Interpreting the Bible can be quite difficult, can't it? If a person takes a certain viewpoint on a verse or a concept they can immediately be accused of not being faithful to the Scriptures. It's vital to remember that although all Christians must agree on primary doctrines such as salvation by grace through faith and the deity of Jesus Christ there are other doctrines such as the timing of the rapture or spiritual gifts where devout Christians may differ on their interpretations.

This principle applies to a person's interpretation of whether or not the Genesis account refers to a literal 24-hour day. Many traditional churches believe the only way to view the creation chronology is as a series of events that took place within six consecutive twenty-four-hour days. However, respected Old Testament scholar Gleason Archer makes this cautionary observation:

> If we were to understand Genesis 1 in a completely literal fashion—which some suppose to be the only proper principle of interpretation if the Bible is truly inerrant and completely trustworthy—then there would be no possibility of reconciliation between modern scientific theory and the Genesis account. But a true and proper belief in the inerrancy of Scripture involves neither a literal nor a figurative rule of interpretation. What it does require is a belief in whatever the biblical author (human and divine) actually meant by the words he used.[61]

It's important to remember that when theologians, scholars, and Christians discuss the exact meaning of the six creation days of Genesis they begin with trying to understand the Hebrew word for "day." The Hebrew word, *yôm* that is translated as "day" has four distinct definitions:

---

[61] Gleason L. Archer, *Encyclopedia of Bible Difficulties* (Grand Rapids, MI: Zondervan Publishing House, 1982), 58.

- Day can refer simply to a part of the daylight hours, such as 6 a.m. to 12 noon.
- Day can refer to all of the daylight hours.
- Day can refer to a twenty-four-hour period.
- Day can refer to a long but finite time period (similar to an age).

Traditionally, Genesis has been understood to teach that the creation events occurred in six consecutive, twenty-four-hour days. A strong case has been made that adding the expressions "morning" and "evening" clearly indicates that the author of Genesis is referring to a twenty-four-day period. However, Hugh Ross makes the following helpful observation:

> In biblical Hebrew, no other word besides *yôm* possesses the meaning of a long but finite period of time. Therefore, if Moses wanted to communicate a creation history consisting of six eons, he would have no other option but to use the word *yôm* to describe those eras.[62]

Therefore, it is feasible that the author's use of the Hebrew word for day might have referred to long, but finite periods of time in which the Creator fashioned the earth into a suitable living environment for humanity. Gleason Archer makes this observation:

> There were six major stages in this work of formation, and these stages are represented by successive days of a week. In this connection it is important to observe that none of the six creative days bears a definite article in the Hebrew text; the translations "the first day," "the second day," etc., are in error. . . . In Hebrew prose of this genre, the definite article was generally used where the noun was intended to be definite; only in poetic style could it be omitted. The same is true with the rest of the six days; they all lack the definite article. Thus they are well adapted to a sequential pattern, rather than to strictly delimited units of time.[63]

---

[62] Hugh Ross, *Navigating Genesis: A Scientist's Journey through Genesis 1-11*, 35.

[63] Gleason L. Archer, *Encyclopedia of Bible Difficulties*, 61.

In the helpful book on this topic, *Genesis One and the Origin of the Earth*, Robert Newman explains his view of the six days of creation:

> The days of Genesis 1 are the twenty-four kind, but they are not consecutive. Furthermore, it is not on these days that all the creative activity takes place. . . . Rather, the days serve some other purpose. It is my suggestion that each day opens a new creative period and therefore each is mentioned in Genesis 1 after the activities of the previous creative period have been described, but before those of the next period are given.[64]

Is the real purpose of Genesis 1 to teach that all creation began just six twenty-four-hour days before Adam was created? If you apply this same perspective to Genesis 2 you'll face some very difficult issues that are hard to resolve. A considerable interval of time must have intervened between the creation of Adam and the creation of Eve. God had given Adam two enormous tasks: the cultivation of the garden and the gigantic task of classifying every species of animals and birds in the Garden of Eden. After these tasks were finished and after Adam once again felt the loneliness of his life, God created Eve. All of this could not have happened within a 24-hour day.

God's creative action began within the structure of a 24-hour day, yet the full extent of His creative activity continues to occur for a long period of time. Each of the seven days of creation represents the beginning of the period of time that God devoted to each of these seminal events of transforming our world into a habitable living space.

TIMELESS TRUTHS FOR A CULTURE THAT TEXTS

The seven days of creation don't have to be a literal 24-hour period of time to be real. They refer to the beginning of key events that transformed Earth to a suitable planet for intelligent life.

---

[64] Robert C. Newman and Herman J. Ecklemann, Jr., *Genesis One and the Origin of the Earth* (Hatfield: Interdisciplinary Biblical Research Institute, 1977), 64-65.

Question 23
What's the Best Explanation for Pre-Historic Man?

After seeing countless articles in National Geographic, headlines in national newspapers, and cable shows dedicated to amazing archaeological finds, it can be very difficult for a Bible-believing Christian to explain the evidence for pre-historic man. My good friend Gail is a sharp thinker who worked for 10 years in the engineering field and regularly had penetrating discussions with her colleagues in the workplace. However, her ultimate challenge came when her elementary age children attended a Christian school and struggled with the questions surrounding pre-historic man. For those who might not know, schools in California (whether they are public or private) must teach the core evolutionary curriculum. Unfortunately, Gail's kids (third and fourth grade) were never given satisfactory answers from their Christian teachers as to the origin of pre-historic man and their relationship with mankind as described in Genesis 1. They would come home from school unsatisfied with the inadequate answers given to them by their teachers. Day after day, they would look for clarification from school but it rarely came. Although they were still quite young—they knew that the answers they had from school simply didn't make sense.

The story of Gail's kids reminds us of the questions that all of us ask from time to time. If God actually created the first man (Adam and Eve), who were these other pre-historic creatures? Doesn't the presence of pre-historic man provide strong evidence for the evolutionary belief that we are simply the descendants of millions of years of evolutionary development? How can I still trust the Biblical account of Adam and Eve when there is physical evidence that human-like creatures existed before the first humans?

Since the Bible doesn't specifically address the issue of pre-historic man, it will not be possible to authoritatively answer this question. However, it is vital that we attempt to integrate what we know about our world with the truths found in the Bible. Fazale Rana's book *Who was Adam?* is a clear and invaluable resource for Christians who wish to have a better explanation for those who wonder whether the truths of the Bible can be logically consistent with the truths found in the scientific world. Here is a summary of his position:

> RTB's (Reason to Believe) biblical creation model considers the hominids found in the fossil record to be animals created by God's direct intervention for His purposes. They existed for a time, and then went extinct. These remarkable creatures walked erect. They also possessed limited intelligence and emotional capacity. Such characteristics allowed them to employ crude tools and even adopt a low level of "culture," much as baboons, gorillas, and chimpanzees do. But while the hominids were created by God's command, they were not spiritual beings made in His image. This status was reserved for human beings.[65]

There are some clear implications that necessarily follow from this particular creation model. Each of these assists the Christian by giving them a little more clarity on the existence of these hominids.

First, the purpose of the Genesis account was to unveil the crowning achievement of God's creative work—humanity. As such, we shouldn't be surprised that these pre-historic hominids were never mentioned in the first two chapters of Genesis. That wasn't the purpose of the Biblical record, and earlier generations of humanity would have struggled to understand who these creatures were since they didn't know of their existence.

Second, similarities between hominids, apes, and mankind don't make an iron-clad case for evolutionary descendants. Rather, it seems to indicate that human beings, as created by God, would share certain physical characteristics with animals and hominids. Remember, similarities can easily be explained by a common creator and not just common descendants. Genesis 2:7 tells us that God "formed the man from the dust of the ground." In other words, Adam and Eve were shaped or fashioned from an available substance or material. However, we are also told in Genesis that the animals and the birds were also created using substances at the disposal of the Creator. If man, animals, and birds were all created from the same substances, it seems reasonable to believe that they might also possess physical similarities.

---

[65] Fazale Rana with Hugh Ross, 50.

Rana makes this observation regarding the use of the Hebrew word meaning "to form," which appears in Genesis 2:7:

> When used to describe God's creative work, *yāşar* emphasizes the forming and shaping of the object. This word choice emphasizes that God created Adam using pre-existing materials. In Genesis 2:19 *yāşar* expresses God's work in forming "out of the ground all the beasts of the field and all the birds of the air." Man, the animals, and birds were all fashioned by the Creator from Earth's raw materials. Being created from the same substances implies physical similarity between humans and animals. Comparative studies should uncover common anatomical, physiological, biochemical, and genetic characteristics.[66]

Third, despite the many similarities that you would expect to find between hominids (pre-historic man) and humans, you have to realize that Scripture is very clear that humans are different in key areas. When God decided to create human beings He did something that had never been done before. God created something new because He placed His image with humanity. Genesis is very clear that when God created the animals and the birds (Genesis 2:19) He did not breathe into them the "breath of life" as He had done with humans (Genesis 2:7). Once again, Rana stresses the importance of this difference:

> People stand apart from animals in that humankind alone received spirit life from God. Only humans concern themselves with morality, purpose, destiny, hope, questions about life and death and judgment after death, and questions about God's existence and character.[67]

Old Testament scholar, Gleason Archer stresses the importance of the difference between pre-historic man and humans when he makes the following observations:

---

[66] Ibid., 49.

[67] Ibid., 49.

> There may have been advanced and intelligent hominids who lived and died before Adam, but they were not created in the image of God. . . . We must reject any interpretation of paleoanthropological data that supposes that a skeletal resemblance establishes that pre-Adamic anthropoids were true human beings in the biblical sense of the term.[68]

> Recent studies of the chimpanzee and the gorilla unquestionably show that subhuman species are capable of tool making, holding hands, patting one another, embracing, and kissing. They are also capable of heartless cruelty to one another, even to cannibalism of their own young. . . . Therefore, evidences of similar intelligence in pre-historic "man" are no decisive proof of humanity in the Adamic sense, nor of moral and spiritual capacity. Hence no strain is put on biblical credibility by these non-Adamic, pre-Adamic races, whatever their antiquity.[69]

Fourth, evolutionists have always believed that *Homo habilis* evolved into the more advanced *Homo erectus*, which evolved into us. Scientists now believe that *habilis* and *erectus* were sister species that overlapped in time. The new fossil evidence reveals an overlap of about 500,000 years during which *Homo habilis* and *Homo erectus* must have co-existed in the Turkana basin area, which is the region of East Africa where the fossils were unearthed. Listen to a member of the world renowned Leakey family, Professor Meave Leakey, has said, "Their co-existence makes it unlikely that *Homo erectus* evolved from *Homo habilis*."

Finally, these issues are very complex and difficult to fully understand because the purpose of the Bible was not to discuss the dinosaurs or pre-historic man. Its purpose was to describe God's redemptive purpose in sending Jesus Christ to Earth in order to restore mankind to a right relationship with a perfect God. Our responsibility is to provide a

---

[68] Gleason L. Archer, *Encyclopedia of Bible Difficulties*, 64.

[69] Gleason L. Archer, 65.

reasonable harmonization between what the Bible reveals and what we have discovered through archaeology. A case can be made (far beyond the scope of this book) that when God made Adam "in His image" directly out of the ground as anatomically modern human, that *Homo erectus* and *Neanderthal* were around already. Adam was "recent" (~100,000 BP from fossil data) and displaced hominids who did not carry the mark of God's image.

TIMELESS TRUTHS FOR A CULTURE THAT TEXTS

Any book is written with a specific purpose in mind. The purpose of the Bible is not to discuss dinosaurs or pre-historic man. It is to describe God's purpose in sending Jesus to Earth.

Question 24
Are the Long Life Spans Described in Genesis Scientifically Possible?

The Guinness World Records confirmed on May of 2016 that Emma Morano of Verbania, Italy, is now the oldest living person at 116 years and 169 days old. In an interview with the NY Times, she revealed that her long life was due to eating three raw eggs a day. In addition, she believed that her amazing longevity was due to her singleness. While we are amazed at the accomplishment of Emma Morano—most people simply shake their heads in disbelief when they read or are told about the incredible life spans of people during the early years of humanity recorded in Genesis. From the unique perspective of the modern thinker, the thought of Methuselah living 969 years (Genesis 5) just doesn't seem possible. It's another example of why people are led to the ultimate conclusion that you can't trust the Bible.

For the Christian who is committed to the accuracy of Scripture, we can't explain this phenomenon simply by claiming that the ancient concept of a "year" must be different than today. First, there is simply no evidence in the Bible or documents outside the Bible that people back in the pre-flood or post-flood era counted years differently than today. Mesopotamian and other ancient cultures used the same basic system as the modern world. Second, if the Biblical concept of a "year" was equivalent to ten modern years, then the student of the Bible is faced with some ludicrous conclusions. For example, Genesis 5:15, 21 records that Mahalalel and Enoch fathered children at the age of 65. If the concept of "year" is not equivalent of the modern notion, then the idea of these men giving birth at a little over 6 years old is ludicrous. Finally, if the concept of "year" was intended to be interpreted differently, then God's prediction of shortening the life spans of people to 120 years (Genesis 6:3) doesn't make any sense.

Of course, after we remove these insufficient explanations for the long life spans of pre-flood people, the committed Christian must still provide some reasonable explanations for why there is such a huge gap between the life spans of Genesis and modern life spans. Remember, our job as defenders of the Bible is to suggest explanations that are either reasonable or plausible. Hugh Ross explains our responsibility this way:

> In certain instances, such as that of human life spans, providing a plausible explanation is the best an interpreter can do. As long as a reasonable scenario exists, one corroborated by evidence and logic, the truthfulness of the account cannot be dismissed.[70]

Christians must provide a plausible explanation for the Biblical long-life spans that seem so very improbable given the current life spans in the modern world.

First, a strict vegetarian diet has the potential to suit a longer life span. It's interesting that God insisted on this form of diet with Adam and Eve and the pre-flood inhabitants. Such a diet would have been necessary for people with an ultra-long life expectancy. Ross makes this observation, "A diet including meat adds higher concentrations of heavy elements in the body (anywhere from 10-10,000 times more than a vegetarian diet)."[71] However, when God announced that humanity in a post-flood world would have a much shorter life expectancy (120 years), He lifted the dietary restrictions and people were allowed to eat animals. It makes sense that God understood the connection between an ultra-long life and the significance of a limited diet consisting of only vegetation.

Second, scientific investigation has revealed a number of factors that limit a healthy life span in today's modern world. Ross itemizes seventeen of these factors but states that a small handful of factors may have special significance when discussing this issue:

> Among them, four alone could realistically account for the great survivability difference: (1) radiation from the decay of radioisotopes (uranium, radium, and thorium for instance) in igneous rocks; (2)

---

[70] Hugh Ross, *Navigating Genesis: A Scientist's Journey Through Genesis 1-11*, 130.

[71] Ibid., 124-125.

> high-energy cosmic radiation; (3) telomerase activity (chromosome shortening); and (4) a high level of meat ingestion.[72]

Two of these factors deserve some additional comments. Scientists tell us that harmful cosmic rays come from outer space via objects like quasars, black holes, neutron stars, and from specialized events like supernova explosions. A team of British and Russian astronomers were able to show the following:

> That virtually all the highest energy heavy nuclei cosmic rays (the most deadly to humans) currently showering Earth could arise from a single supernova—as yet unidentified—in the recent past (less than 100,000 years ago) relatively near (closer than 3,000 light-years away) to our solar system.[73]

Additional research seems to indicate that the only supernova that fits all the parameters is the Monogem Ring. The age and proximity of this super nova seems consistent with the Biblical assertion that God may have used deadly cosmic rays to shorten human life spans in the post-flood world. Christian scientists like Hugh Ross think that it is plausible that these deadly cosmic rays hadn't yet arrived during Noah's time, which accounts for the extremely long life spans.

Scientists also tell us that one of the most important life span factors comes from inside our bodies and not outside. Listen to Hugh Ross' explanation of what happens inside our body:

> As in all complex organisms, our cells can undergo only a certain number of replications. For cells that make up differentiated tissues, organs, and appendages (the somatic cells), the "telemore" region of its chromosome is incompletely replicated during cell division. Thus, each chromosome becomes shorter and shorter as cell division continues. Eventually, chromosomes become so short that important genes fail to get replicated. . . . So the organs, tissues, and

---

[72] Ibid., 125.

[73] Ibid., 127.

> appendages can no longer perform their life-essential functions, and death occurs. What this telomere shortening means for humans today is that no matter how healthy a person's lifestyle or how radiation-free a person's environment, he or she will not live beyond about 120 years.[74]

In the pre-flood era, the telomerase activity could have been much higher. However, when the radiation levels increased due to the impact of deadly cosmic rays, it's possible that God may have intervened by limiting telomerase activity in an attempt to protect the exposure of humans with long life spans.

Finally, it's possible that God intentionally limited the life spans of human (post Genesis 5) as a protective umbrella against the increasing evilness of the world. Genesis 6:3 tells us, "Then the LORD said, "My Spirit will not contend with humans forever, for they are mortal; their days will be a hundred and twenty years.". Consider the observations of Ross:

> From what we observe of human behavior, shorter life spans serve to limit the destructive impact of human selfishness, greed, and lawlessness. Individuals bent on violence can harm or destroy a great many people in a 900-year lifetime, and their spiritual malignancy tends to spread like a cancer. The lengthy life span of pre-flood peoples may help explain why only one family among the entire human race was deemed salvageable by the time of Noah's six-hundredth year.[75]

This chapter has illustrated one of the realities a person faces when reading through the book of Genesis. There are many issues where the present evidence of science is not sufficient to provide absolute certainty for Biblical positions. Simply put, we can't explain all the issues we find in Scripture. Clearly, we don't have the ability to grasp the supernatural power of God. In addition, it's possible that there are scientific reasons that could explain these long life spans but they have yet been revealed.

---

[74] Ibid., 128.

[75] Ibid., 129.

It's also possible that science will reveal something in the future that might explain these seeming impossibilities. In the midst of these uncertainties, it's helpful to remember all the different issues where science (Big Bang) or history (Red Sea discoveries) have provided compelling evidence for the accuracy of the Biblical account.

TIMELESS TRUTHS FOR A CULTURE THAT TEXTS

We can't explain all the issues we find in Scripture—especially the issue of the extreme old ages revealed in the book of Genesis. It's possible that there are scientific reasons that have not yet been revealed or that we simply can't fathom the design and power of God.

Question 25
Was the Genesis Flood Local or Global?

In the Hollywood movie *Noah*, God orders Noah (Russell Crowe) to build an ark large enough to hold his wife and family. God had decided that mankind had become too sinful and must be wiped off the earth. Although it was great cinematic entertainment, the underlying issue in the minds of many skeptics was probably a very simple one—did the Genesis flood actually happen? Just think about what your skeptical friend might have been thinking as they watched *Noah*. How could water have spread over the entire world? What forces could have created that much water? Is it possible that rain could cover the highest mountain range? It's not hard to see how both skeptics and some Christians might struggle with understanding how water could cover the entire globe.

I wish you knew my friend Derick, a white-collar professional in his 50's with two children. Derick has always been intrigued by mysteries like the Bermuda Triangle or T.V. shows like the X-Files. He's fascinated by the complexity of our world and the search for truth. He's not shy about investigating anything with drama, confusion, or debate. Derick takes this same attitude as he explores the relationship between science and faith. As my friend looks at the controversy surrounding the Genesis account of the flood he has learned to take a fresh look at the issue. Despite the complexity, he's confident he'll find the truth.

The purpose of this chapter is to reexamine one of the most contentious issues within the modern Church. Please don't misunderstand me. I firmly believe that God, if He wished too, could cover the entire planet with water. However, I think it is possible that the flood described by the Bible may have been worldwide, or universal, without covering the globe.

The Bible uses the term "world" in three different ways. It can refer to the entire globe as created by God (Hebrews 1:2); it can refer to the people who inhabit the earth (John 3:16); or it can refer to the evil system that confronts the Christian on a regular basis (1 John 2:15). When a modern thinker uses the word "world" we think of a truly global environment where we can travel to any location on the planet. However, previous generations would have looked at the world in a much different way. The world or the globe would have consisted of every place inhabited by people—not necessarily the entire physical planet. In other words, they would have looked at the "world" as the place where people lived, not every inch of Planet Earth.

With this important distinction in mind, I think we can make an effective and reasonable defense of the Genesis Flood to our skeptical friends. The flood was global in the sense that it impacted everyone in the world. However, it was regional in the sense that it didn't cover the entire planet—only the world that was inhabited by people. The following are some reasons for this viewpoint.

First, Biblical references for worldwide events regularly point to an area less than the entire surface of the Earth. In addition to the Flood, there are the six Scriptural references to worldwide events:

- Joseph feeding the whole world (Genesis 41-42).
- Foreign leaders seeking Solomon's wisdom (1 Kings 4).
- Decree from Caesar Augustus (Luke 2).
- Arrival of various visitors at Pentecost (Acts 2).
- Paul's commendation to the Christians in Rome (Romans 1).
- Paul's letter to the Christians in Colossae (Colossians 1).

Based upon the context or a simple understanding of the author's intent, these references could not have meant the entire globe. In each example, the concept of worldwide referred to the reach of a government or a certain geographic area during that period of time. As we attempt to interpret the Genesis Flood we use the same principle. Rana makes the following observation:

> Each of these biblical references to a worldwide occurrence points to an area less than Earth's entire surface or entire land area. Therefore, phrases such as "the entire heavens" and "the face of the earth" in the context of Noah's flood may also refer to an area or region smaller that the whole of Earth's surface. . . . Rather than signify anything about geography, this repetition more likely

> emphasizes that the flood impacted all of humanity. Once again, if humans had not yet begun to occupy all of Earth's landmasses, the flood could be worldwide, or universal, without covering the globe.[76]

Second, the book of Genesis indicates that God had always intended for humanity to fully populate Earth. However, on several occasions people failed to spread out and populate the earth. God commanded Adam and Eve to multiply and fill the earth. God repeats this same command to Noah after the flood (Genesis 9). In fact, we can see that humanity was still defying the wishes of God several generations after Noah when the peoples of the world gathered at the Tower of the Babel (Genesis 11). This is yet another evidence that humanity, at this point, was relatively restricted to one geographical area. In other words, the "world" in the early days of Genesis simply did not refer to the entire globe as it does today.

Third, human origins seem to have their beginning somewhere in or near North Africa. Rana states, "the best scholarship places the garden's location in Mesopotamia, with the possibility that it extended into northern and eastern Africa."[77] If this is correct, then it also seems likely that the flood occurred in the general area of the Mesopotamian region. Several truths can be deduced from this one fact. If the ark were floating in the Persian Gulf or on top of two hundred feet of water deep in the vast Mesopotamian plains, Noah would not have been able to see anything other than water. Genesis 7:19 describes Noah's inability to see anything but water, from horizon to horizon, from his viewpoint on the ark's upper deck. As stated by Hugh Ross:

> His view would have been limited by Earth's curvature, by atmospheric conditions, and by his aging eyes, among other factors. Those who travel through California's San Joaquin Valley (much narrower than the Mesopotamian valley) typically cannot see

---

[76] Hugh Ross, *Navigating Genesis: A Scientist's Journey through Genesis 1-11,* 147.

[77] Fazale Rana with Hugh Ross, 45.

> the towering peaks to the east or the coastal range to the west, at least not from the valley's center.[78]

Fourth, many Christians believe that that the Genesis Flood must have covered the entire planet because Genesis 8:4 tells us that Noah's Ark came to rest on Mount Ararat. Since Mount Ararat has an elevation of 16,945 feet above sea level, people simply assume that the Genesis Flood must have covered all the high mountains of the earth. The Hebrew words for "cover" and "high mountains" which are used in Genesis 7:19-21 do not necessarily imply that the flood must have covered every mountain in the entire world. The Hebrew word for mountains has a wide range of meaning. It can imply a mountain where the path of ascent is steep, a small hill that can be climbed in an afternoon walk, or anything in between those extremes. When we are told that "the ark came to rest on the mountains of Ararat" this could easily refer to the entire Ararat range with elevations ranging from the hundreds to the thousands of feet. According to the Genesis account, Noah's Ark could have come to rest anywhere within this region—not simply on the top of Mount Ararat.

Fifth, if the flood occurred in a specific geographic area, this might explain why God was able to significantly remove the flood waters. Water that filled a flat region like Mesopotamia would naturally flow toward the sea. However, a wind like the one described in Genesis 8 would not only accelerate the drainage of the water but also speed the natural evaporation of the water.

Sixth, Genesis 7:11-12 tells us the sources for the Genesis Flood when it says the waters came from "the springs of the great deep" and "the floodgates of the heavens." It seems clear that the springs of the deep refer to subterranean reservoirs or aquifers. Hugh Ross relates this to the region during Noah's day:

> Like most desert plains, the Gulf Oasis and Mesopotamia possessed geological features that favor formation of large aquifers.

---

[78] Ibid., 150-151.

> Certain geologic events can bring that water to the surface. And, while rain falls only rarely in Mesopotamia and the Persian Gulf region, an "act of God" could bring about the 40-days torrential downpour Genesis records.[79]

Finally, God's judgment is focused on the presence of sin. He has no need to extend his judgment randomly to geographic areas that don't deserve it. The concept of God's judgment relates directly to the issue of the Genesis flood. If the purpose of the flood was to judge the presence of sin in an entirely evil population, then only that portion of the globe that was inhabited by people would have been destroyed. Hugh Ross makes the point this way:

> If people remained only in the region of Mesopotamia and the Persian Gulf, only that region would have to be flooded. Whatever area it covered, the flood must still be "worldwide," given that people, not the globe, defined "world" (until a much later area). Any flood that exterminates all humans and their soulish animals—except those on board Noah's vessel—would be considered worldwide and would achieve God's purpose in pouring out judgment to cleanse the earth of reprobate defilement.[80]

TIMELESS TRUTHS FOR A CULTURE THAT TEXTS

The Genesis Flood was universal in that all humanity was impacted by it. It's possible that it was geographically limited because humanity at that time was restricted to a certain region of the world.

---

[79] Ibid., 152.

[80] Ibid., 144.

Question 26
Isn't Evolution a Proven Fact?

Famous atheist, Richard Dawkins stressed the importance of the evolutionary theory developed by Charles Darwin when he said the following:

> An atheist before Darwin could have said, following Hume: "I have no explanation for complex biological design. All I know is that God isn't a good explanation, so we must wait and hope that somebody comes up with a better one." I can't help feeling that such a position, though logically sound, would have left one feeling pretty unsatisfied, and that although atheism might have been logically tenable before Darwin, Darwin made it possible to be an intellectually fulfilled atheist.[81]

Dr. J. William Schopf, director of the UCLA's Center for the Study of Evolution and the Origin of Life raises the stakes even higher when he makes this statement:

> Evolution is the GUT (GRAND UNIFYING THEORY) of biology. It is the bedrock principle of our scientific understanding of the natural laws that govern life. Furthermore, it is logically necessary for life's survival in a changing world environment. To deny this scientific principle is analogous to believing that the earth is the center of the universe![82]

Of all the issues that face the Christian, there is probably no single issue that has more inertia within our culture than people's belief that evolution best explains the origins of humanity. Although a treatment of all the facts involved in the creation and evolution debate is beyond the scope

---

[81] Richard Dawkins, *The Blind Watchmaker: Why the Evidence of Evolution Reveals A Universe Without Design* (New York: W. & W. Norton Company, 1986), 6.

[82] Sylvia Mader and Michael Windelspecht, *Inquiry into Life* (New York; McGraw Hill, 2014), 5.

of this chapter, I think it's helpful to clarify a handful of issues related to the topic of evolution.

First, it's important to remember that evolution is not just an explanation for how natural selection acting on random variations can explain the wide diversity of plants and animals. Evolution embraces the concept of philosophical materialism—the belief that matter is all there is and that there is no immaterial or spiritual component in our universe. As a result of this belief, it's not surprising that evolution is part of the foundation for modern atheism.

Second, for years it was the commonly held belief that the universe was eternal. As such, there was no need for a divine creator. The proposal of the theory of evolution by Charles Darwin simply provided an explanation for how humanity came into existence without God. However, the Big Bang was a scientific breakthrough that stunned the scientific community and challenged naturalism. If the universe had no beginning, no cause is required. But if the universe had a beginning, there must have been a transcendent and eternal source (God) who brought it into existence. When the Big Bang was confirmed in 1992 (COBE Explorer), the implications for the theory of evolution were quite evident. Sir Arthur Eddington expressed it years earlier, "Philosophically, the notion of a beginning of the present order of Nature is repugnant. . . . I should like to find a genuine loophole. . . . We must allow evolution an infinite time to get started."[83]

Third, for many years there has been growing evidence in the universe that our world did not begin to exist merely by chance but was the direct by-product of a superb intelligence. In the 1950s, eminent physicist and agnostic Fred Holye made some surprising admissions, "A commonsense interpretation of the facts suggests that a super intellect has monkeyed with physics, as well as chemistry and biology, and that

---

[83] Hugh Ross, *The Creator and the Cosmos: How the Greatest Scientific Discoveries of the Century Reveal God*, 51.

there are no blind forces worth speaking about in nature."[84] In reviewing the growing list of 200+ fine-tuning factors that demonstrate our universe could not have come into existence by mere chance or accident, noted theoretical physicist Paul Davies described the fine-tuning of the universe as "the most compelling evidence for an element of cosmic design."[85]

Despite this evidence, evolutionists like Richard Dawkins believes that, "Biology is the study of complicated things that give the appearance of having been designed for appearance."[86] Nobel laureate Francis Crick, who was the co-discoverer of the structure of DNA, wrote, "Biologists must constantly keep in mind that what they see was not designed, but rather, evolved."[87] Of course, these viewpoints are clearly contradictory to the viewpoint of Scripture, which believes that all of creation reflect the personal handiwork of God (Psalm 8:3-4).

Fourth, if Darwin's theory of evolution is true, a person would expect to find clear fossil evidence for the concept of common descent. In other words, the fossils should demonstrate a continuous line of creatures with major groups of organisms blending smoothly from one group to another via many transitional forms. Charles Darwin made his own admission regarding the fossil record:

> The number of intermediate varieties, which have formerly existed on earth, {must} be truly enormous. Why then is not every geological formation and every stratum full of such intermediate links? Geology assuredly does not reveal any such finely graduated organic chain; and this, perhaps, is the most obvious and gravest objection, which can be urged against my theory.[88]

---

[84] Fred Hoyle in Paul Davies, *The Accidental Universe* (Cambridge: Cambridge University Press, 1982), 118.

[85] Paul Davies, *The Accidental Universe*, 189.

[86] Richard Dawkins, *The Blind Watchmaker*, 1.

[87] Francis Crick, *What Mad Pursuit* (New York: Basic Books, 1988), 138.

[88] Charles Darwin, *The Origin of the Species* (Cambridge, MA: Harvard University Press, 1964), 280.

Fifth, the complexity of a human organism could not have been anticipated during the time of Charles Darwin. His understanding of the human cell was rudimentary at best; it was nothing like our present understanding of the complexity of DNA and the amazing wealth of information found within every human cell. This reveals another crucial insight into the inherent weakness of evolutionary theory. Darwin believed in numerous, successive, slight modifications. However, every one of these small steps must enhance the organism's ability to survive and reproduce without negatively impacting the organism. What a lot of people don't realize is that Darwin expressed reservation about the foundation of his evolutionary theory when he said, "If it could be demonstrated that any complex organ existed which could not possibly have been formed by numerous, successive, slight modifications, my theory would absolutely break down."[89]

Lehigh University biochemist Michael Behe has shown that what Darwin feared is actually a reality. In his book *Darwin's Black Box*, Behe describes the concept of irreducible complexity and why it provides clear evidence against the theory of evolution. Behe describes this concept and its importance in the following fashion:

> By irreducible complexity I mean a single system which is composed of several interacting parts that contribute to the basic function, and where the removal of any one of the parts causes the system to effectively cease functioning. An irreducibly complex system cannot be produced gradually by slight, successive modifications of a precursor system, since any precursor to an irreducibly complex system is by definition nonfunctional. . . . It is almost universally conceded that such a sudden event would be irreconcilable with the gradualism Darwin envisioned.[90]

---

[89] Charles Darwin, *The Origin of the Species*, 189.

[90] Michael Behe in David DeWolf, John West, Casey Luskin, and Jonathan Witt, *Traipsing Into Evolution: Intelligent Design and the Kitzmiller vs. Dover Decision* (Seattle: Discovery Institute Press, 2006), 38-39.

Sixth, the issue of the origin of life on our planet is extremely problematic for those who embrace naturalism (evolution). For centuries, philosophers and scientists believed in a universe that was eternal—providing an endless amount of time for life to originate. However, growing evidence shows that life had to originate on Earth within a much quicker time frame. Hugh Ross explains the thinking behind this observation:

> It leaves no room for doubt (based on dating of lunar craters and on comparisons of craters on the moon, Mars, and Mercury) that Earth and other bodies close to the sun experienced heavy bombardment by meteors, comets, asteroids, and dust in their early history. From 4.25 until 3.8 billion years ago, the bombardment of Earth was so intense that no life could have survived it. From 3.8 until 3.5 billion years ago the bombardment gradually decreased to its present comparatively low level. But during those 300 million years at least thirty life-exterminating impacts must have occurred. . . . They show that life sprang up on Earth (and re-sprang) in what could be called geologic instants, periods of ten-million years or less. . . . From the perspective of our life span, a ten-million-year window may seem long, but it is impossibly short to those seeking to explain life's origins without divine input.[91]

These six observations seem to reveal that evolution, as the philosophical backbone of naturalism, is increasingly unlikely as an explanation for the beginning and fine tuning of the universe, the origin of life, the fossil record, and the complexity of organisms.

TIMELESS TRUTHS FOR A CULTURE THAT TEXTS

Evolution is not the most likely explanation for our world. The beginning of the universe, its fine-tuning, the complexity of the human organism, and the origin of life all show it's not true.

---

[91] Hugh Ross, *The Creator and the Cosmos: How the Greatest Scientific Discoveries of the Century Reveal God*, 138.

Issues of Faith

Richard Dawkins, who is one of the most vocal and famous atheists in our culture expresses the challenge facing the person of faith in our modern culture. Listen to two of his observations: "Science replaces private prejudice with verifiable evidence. . . . The truth is more magical than any myth or made-up mystery or miracle. Science has its own magic: the magic of reality."[92]

Time and time again, the opinion shapers in our culture have told people that the only things that can be trusted as "fact" are things that can be determined by the five senses—things that science can teach us! Science gives us facts and real truth. Morality gives us preferences. Religion gives us opinions. Facts can be trusted—opinions can't.

Christians live in a thoroughly skeptical age that threatens our spiritual journey. How many times have you heard that faith is illogical? How often have you not known what to say when a critic has compared your belief in Jesus to trusting in Santa Claus or the Easter Bunny? Our skeptical culture routinely views faith as an emotional or illogical action. Faith is ridiculed and viewed as the opposite of scientific truth.

---

92 Richard Dawkins, *The Magic of Reality: How We Know What's Really True* (New York: Free Press, 2011), 257.

Each of the questions in this section relates to the issue of faith. Each of these responses are predicated on the Scriptural teaching that God has an important role for faith (Hebrews 11:6) and an important role for reason (1 Peter 3:15). We should try our very best to hold these Scriptural priorities in balance.

Question 27
Is Religious Faith Reasonable?

During a lecture addressing the central ask of world evangelism, Charles Malik expressed this harsh assessment about the American form of Christianity. Listen to his frank admission:

> I must be frank with you: the greatest danger confronting American evangelical Christianity is the danger of anti-intellectualism. The mind in its greatest and deepest reaches is not cared for enough. . . . Does the evangelical mode of thinking have the slightest chance of becoming the dominant mode in the great universities of Europe and America that stamp our entire civilization with their spirit and ideas?[93]

Clearly, the modern church has not always placed the correct emphasis on Christian thought. In a world that is increasingly skeptical, the modern church has not prepared itself to answer the question of whether the Christian faith is reasonable. Too many Christians have fallen asleep at the wheel. Many churches have abandoned any focus on the intellectual foundation of our faith. All too often, the attention is solely placed on living the Christian life, understanding the Bible better, or being a more dedicated follower of Jesus Christ. Don't get me wrong—these are very important issues. However, the church has contributed to a religious climate in which too many Christians haven't even considered whether our faith is reasonable or whether it is even important to ask the question.

Although we hold faith in the highest regard, this doesn't necessarily mean that there are not solid reasons to buttress our beliefs. Faith in Christianity is not the same as faith in the Easter Bunny or Santa Claus. Great protestant intellectual and philosopher Alvin Plantinga states it this way:

---

[93] Charles Malik in William Lane Craig, *Reasonable Faith: Christian Truth and Apologetics* (Wheaton: Crossway Books, 1994), xii.

> Christian faith is not at all like a leap in the dark. It is not a matter of believing something on the basis of scanty evidence. Faith is not to be contrasted with knowledge. . . . It just is a certain kind of knowledge, and knowledge of truths of the greatest importance.[94]

Unfortunately, many believers either don't know the relationship between faith and reason or how to respond to those who claim that the Christian faith is unreasonable. We must win the battle against the notion that religious faith is opposed to reason. Religious faith is not at odds with reason.

It's vital that we attempt to reclaim the intellectual high ground as it relates to discussing the Christian faith. Faith is not the logical opposite of reason. Faith is built upon a reasonable foundation of evidence. Faith simply asks us to place our confidence in things we don't yet fully comprehend.

TIMELESS TRUTHS FOR A CULTURE THAT TEXTS

Faith in Christianity is not the same as faith in the Easter Bunny or Santa Claus. It's built upon reasonable evidence.

---

[94] Alvin Plantinga and Michael Tooley, *Knowledge of God* (Malden: Blackwell Publishing, 2008), 9.

Question 28
Can Christianity Be Proved with Certainty?

In the early years of my Christian experience two things were my constant companions. First, I had an insatiable appetite to share my faith in Jesus Christ. I would go up to Hollywood and Vine on Saturday nights to engage people in conversation. I was eager to share with friends, acquaintances, and strangers why it was so essential for them to have a personal relationship with Christ. It was a time of unparalleled excitement. Second, I also had a quest for more and more knowledge about my faith. I read a lot of books and attended conferences dedicated to defending the faith. I was driven by a simple hope that I would be able to provide absolute certainty as I presented the Christian faith to people around me. I reasoned that if Christianity was really true there had to be absolute proof.

Some years later, I realized a greater truth. I would never find absolute certainty because God is interested in people expressing an element of faith as they seek Him. God could have easily overwhelmed people with His presence or with regular miraculous events, but He's not interested in compelling people to believe in Him. God must honor the dignity of free will that He has given to all humanity.

It's not that Christianity is unreasonable. In fact, Christianity is supremely reasonable. Christian thinker and apologist Ravi Zacharias makes this timeless observation, "God has given enough reason in this world to make faith in him a most reasonable thing. But he has left out enough to make it impossible to live by sheer reason and observation alone."[95] The Christian faith dovetails with the evidence that God has left all around us. He has left us sufficient evidence apart from Scripture that He is powerful (Romans 1:18-20), moral (Romans 2:15), and good (Acts 14:17). In addition, He has left signs of His handiwork that can be determined by modern science and history. Scripture also provides evidence of the superior claims of Jesus of Nazareth and the miracles

---

[95] Ravi Zacharias, *The Real Face of Atheism* (Ada: Baker Books, 2004), 112.

that have confirmed the absolute truthfulness of the Christian faith (John 20:31).

However, faith does require us to believe things without absolute certainty. There are many things in life that we must place our trust in without absolute certainty. Atheists and Christians both face this reality. Neither the atheist nor the Christian can claim absolute certainty on whether God does or doesn't exist. Evolutionists can't provide absolute naturalistic evidence for the beginning of life. Christians can't go back in time to observe the Virgin Birth to determine the supernatural process at work. There is no iron-clad scientific truth written in the sky that will put these issues to rest. In this sense, both the atheist and the Christian must exercise faith at certain moments in life.

As I have grown in Christian maturity I have gained a powerful appreciation for the dignity of free will. God has given every person who has ever stepped on this planet the ability to choose to seek Him or to resist knowledge of God's plan for their life. God has designed free will, in part, so that we might freely pursue and choose God. Absolute certainty would eliminate the dignity of free will. Although we would love to see facts and evidence that would absolutely convince even the most ardent skeptic, we must honor the concept of free will that God has given humanity.

For many of our skeptical friends, the transition from probable to certainty is very difficult. The story of Sheldon Vanauken, who studied at Yale and Oxford and came to faith in Christ through the influence of C.S. Lewis, provides stunning clarity about what it takes for a "leap of faith." His words stand not only as a haunting reminder of what is at stake, but of what is possible:

> There is a gap between the probable and the proved. How was I to cross it? If I were to stake my whole life on the risen Christ, I wanted proof. I wanted certainty. I wanted to see him eat a bit of fish. I wanted letters of fire across the sky. I got none of these. And I continued to hang about on the edge of the gap. . . . It was a question of whether I was to accept him—or reject. My God! There was a gap behind me as well! Perhaps the leap to acceptance was a horrifying gamble—but what of the leap to rejection? There might be

no certainty that Christ was God—but, by God, there was no certainty that he was not. This was not to be borne. I could not reject Jesus. There was only one thing to do once I had seen the gap behind me. I turned away from it, and flung myself over the gap toward Jesus.[96]

TIMELESS TRUTHS FOR A CULTURE THAT TEXTS

Christianity does not provide absolute certainty because God has created humanity with the dignity of free will—the ability to choose to trust in the evidence that surrounds them.

[96] Alister E. McGrath, *Intellectuals Don't Need God & Other Modern Myths: Building Bridges to Faith Through Apologetics* (Grand Rapids: Zondervan, 1993), 59.

Question 29
Is It Wrong to Doubt?

Doubt is a silent killer. Churches are filled with people who silently struggle with issues of doubt. They feel alone or abandoned by those around them. Over the past several years, I've developed a wonderful friendship with a millennial by the name of Jason. Jason is a non-practicing Catholic who works in the banking industry. He's funny, engaging, and open to religious conversation. In talking to him about his life within the church, I was heartbroken by his story of how his spiritual journey hit a significant obstacle when he was a youth leader within the Catholic Church. During a crucial time in his life, he faced a lot of doubts and questions but he never got solid answers. The answers to his questions seemed to be scripted without any real sensitivity to the struggles of a youth leader. Folks, Jason's inability to get answers at an important juncture in his life is one of the reasons why he's drifted within his Catholic faith. Although he still embraces many of the core truths of his faith, Jason is interested in making his beliefs his own—not merely believing truths that he's told to embrace.

When I speak to someone who has a religious background like Jason, I've found it extraordinarily helpful to simply tell the story of the predecessor and forerunner to Jesus Christ. In the twilight of his career, John the Baptist, who was one of the true giants of the faith, found himself in jail. He had heard the incredible accounts of the ministry of Jesus, yet he was waiting for more tangible signs of the arrival of the kingdom of God. In that moment of isolation, John asked a couple of his disciples to ask Jesus a simple question, "Are you the one who was to come, or should we expect someone else (Luke 7:20)?"

Here's the simple reality: John wasn't sure. John had questions. The great John the Baptist had a genuine moment of doubt regarding whether Jesus was the intended Messiah. However, in John's moment of weakness and insecurity Jesus didn't rebuke John, nor did he chastise him. Listen to His words, "Go back and report to John what you have seen and heard: The blind receive sight, the lame walk, those who have leprosy are cured, the deaf hear, the dead are raised, and the good news is preached to the poor (Luke 7:22)."

By reminding John of the miracles He was performing, Jesus showed that He was fulfilling prophecy. Jesus didn't insist on blind faith. He gave John the Baptist evidence designed to bolster John's faith.

Here's what this means for the Christian journey of faith. In a world that lacks certainty and where social media places the spotlight on a wide variety of opinions, it's only reasonable to expect that many Christians will struggle with doubt. Christians are bombarded with issues 24/7. The views of Christianity are regularly attacked in public media. The church must be prepared to deal with doubt. We shouldn't be shocked. We shouldn't interpret doubt as an absence of faith. We must provide the modern-day Christian with the tools to deal with and disarm doubt. This is one of the great callings of our generation. We must deal with doubt head on.

I am no stranger to the experience of doubt. I've had moments of doubt in which I've intellectually struggled with the issues of hell and evil. I've also had disappointing seasons when I have faced situations that caused me to doubt God's providence and goodness. Here are a couple of suggestions that have personally helped me to gain the upper hand in those seasons when I was overwhelmed with doubt.

First, I've learned the importance of trying to resolve issues of doubt one at a time. I focus on whatever issue is most troublesome and glean insights from quality authors or mature Christians until I feel comfortable enough to provide a reasonable answer. My goal is not to find certainty or to totally remove any further questions that will come to my mind. I am simply trying to get to the point where I can feel at peace that my viewpoint on the particular issue is more reasonable than the atheistic/agnostic viewpoint on life.

Second, I've also found it very helpful to verbalize doubts. A couple of years ago, I was speaking at a church on the topic of *How to Disarm Your Doubt*. Nothing prepared me for the moment at the end of the service when a middle-aged woman approached me in tears and whispered to me, "That's the first time that someone in the church ever told me that it was okay to have doubts!" As I listened to her story, I had difficulty holding my emotions in check until I started my drive home.

I've never been hesitant to admit that there are issues that bother me as a thinking Christian. Of course, as a public speaker dedicated to defending the Christian faith, I can't share all my personal doubts in a public forum. However, I can write in such a way that validates the difficulty of certain issues and the importance of providing reasonable answers for people inside and outside the church. I also try to maintain openness with trusted associates, family, and friends when I am troubled with certain issues. Verbalizing my doubts and questions helps me gain a greater perspective and a more hopeful outlook on the particular issue.

Doubt used to be a demon in my life. The pursuit of certainty was an impossible standard that I thought I would never attain. Fortunately, I am no longer overwhelmed by doubt. I look doubt straight in the eyes and realize that it is not fatal—it's part of everyone's emotional and spiritual journey.

TIMELESS TRUTHS FOR A CULTURE THAT TEXTS

Everyone faces moments of doubt. It's what you do in those moments that make all the difference. Doubt can define or destroy, or you can disarm it.

Theological Issues

C.S. Lewis, who was one of the foundational Christian minds that shaped the 20th century had this to say about the importance of theology:

> Theology is practical: especially now. In the old days, when there was less education and discussion, perhaps it was possible to get on with a very few simple ideas about God. But it is not so now. Everyone reads, everyone hears things discussed. Consequently, if you do not listen to theology, that will not mean that you have no ideas about God. It will mean that you have a lot of wrong ones—bad, muddled, out-of-date ideas.[97]

The modern Church lives in a time when there are a lot of wrong and bad ideas about God. These ideas exist inside and outside the church and are thwarting the spiritual journey of far too many people. Unfortunately, the church is not preparing the next generation of people to cope intellectually with these concepts. Preaching calendars are very full of self-help and feel-good messages that never really empower believers to think through and defend their faith.

---

[97] C.S. Lewis, *The Complete C.S. Lewis Signature Classic* (New York: HarperCollins, 2002), 128.

Tragically, if we don't provide Christians with the tools to think through theological issues, rest assured that there will be skeptics who will raise these issues in an attempt to confuse or derail a person's faith. Jesus spoke about the importance of theological truth when He said, "If you hold to my teaching, you are truly my disciples. Then you will know the truth, and the truth will set you free (John 8:31-32)."

Question 30
Can You Lose Your Salvation?

Years ago, while I was a student at Cal State Long Beach, I tried to run a six-minute mile. I knew I had to run every lap of the track in 90 seconds. The first three laps were very difficult, but the last lap was absolute torture. My legs were burning, I was gasping for breath, and with every stride I wanted to quit. However, I finished in just under six minutes. For the record, I've never done it since. I had a similarly agonizing journey as I tried to finish my doctoral dissertation in the face of an imposing deadline. I spent three seventeen-hour days in the library going page by page to find errors and to re-submit certain sections that didn't meet the approval of my advisors. Just when I was convinced that I couldn't concentrate for another go-around, my dissertation was accepted and I crossed the finish line.

God knows that a person's spiritual journey from Point A to Point Z is very difficult and agonizing. Our spiritual life is fraught with intense roadblocks, challenges, sin, and lack of faith. Sometimes these challenges can cause us to doubt whether or not we are really saved or whether we will make it to the finish line. Some Christians struggle throughout their lives with the question of assurance. They doubt whether or not they are really saved. They question whether or not they can lose their salvation. They receive Christ again and again in hopes of covering their spiritual bases.

Fortunately, I believe that God has made a commitment to walk with us during our spiritual journey until the moment we arrive in heaven. C.S. Lewis got it absolutely right when he said:

> Make no mistake, He says, if you let Me, I will make you perfect. The moment you put yourself in My hands, that is what you are in for. Nothing less, or other, than that. . . . Whatever suffering it may cost you in your earthly life, . . . whatever it costs Me, I will never rest, nor let you rest, until you are literally perfect.[98]

---

[98] C.S. Lewis, *Mere Christianity* (New York: Macmillan, 1952), 158.

Scripture teaches that once God places within us the marks of our new identity we are forever His. The question of assurance is really a question of identity. Our spiritual identity tells us, "once His; always His." There are numerous Scriptures that demonstrate the security of a person's salvation. Philippians 1:6 tells us that "He who began a good work will carry it on to completion until the day of Christ Jesus." John 6:39 says, "I shall lose none of all that he has given me, but raise them up at the last day." Ephesians 4:30 promises that we have been "sealed for the day of redemption." Jesus promised His disciples, "I give them eternal life, and they shall never perish: no one can snatch them out of my hand (John 10:28)." The Apostle Paul reassured believers by saying, "Neither height nor depth, nor anything else in all creation, will be able to separate us from the love of God that is in Christ Jesus our Lord (Romans 8:39)." In his doxology, the Apostle John affirmed this by saying, "To him who is able to keep you from falling and to present you before his glorious presence without fault and with great joy (Jude 24)."

Of course, there are a handful of difficult passages that seem to indicate that a Christian might be able to lose his or her salvation (Hebrews 6:4-6; John 15:6; Matthew 24:13). Although it is beyond the scope of this chapter to explore these passages in detail there are two principles that are helpful in resolving these issues. First, no one can understand whether or not a person has truly been born again. Only God can determine whether a person is a child of God. From our limited perspective, we simply can't determine whether or not a person who abandons the Christian faith (loses their salvation) was ever truly a believer. Second, it's important to remember that there is a difference between the apparent falling away of the genuine believer and the genuine falling away of the apparent believer. The difficult passages may simply be describing someone who is not truly a believer.

I've discovered that one single verse shines tremendous insight into this issue. In Paul's Epistle to the Romans we read the following, "29 For those God foreknew he also predestined to be conformed to the likeness of his Son, that he might be the firstborn among many brothers. 30 And those he predestined, he also called; those he called, he also justified; those he justified, he also glorified (Romans 8:30)."

Five very significant theological terms are packed within the space of two verses. Once Paul begins talking about God's actions toward a group of people in eternity past, he continues to talk about the same group of people through the end of our life. In other words, no one gets dropped from the initial group of people.

- Foreknowledge: This refers to God's gracious choice of people to experience salvation. God's choice precedes our knowledge of Him (1 Peter 1:1,2).
- Predestined: This refers to God's divine decision that the elect would be conformed to the very image of Christ (Romans 8:29; 12:2).
- Called: This refers to the specific time within a person's lifetime when God calls him or her to hear and respond to the good news of Jesus Christ. It may be helpful to think of "calling" and "conversion" as two sides of the same coin (Romans 10:9).
- Justified: This is the moment when God graciously grants us the righteousness of Christ (Romans 5:1).
- Glorified: This is the divine decision to glorify believers when they arrive in heaven. It's the final step of the process during which we receive new bodies along with a new heavenly home (1 Corinthians 15:51-53).

What does all this mean? It's really simple! Those who are objects of God's foreknowledge will also be the objects of His predestination, His calling, His justification, and His glorification. In other words, once a person is the object of God's saving faith; no one drops through the cracks—no one. Once a person is part of God's eternal plan they will stay within His grasp until they touch foot on the soil of heaven. God placed His love upon the Christian from eternity past and He will never let go.

TIMELESS TRUTHS FOR A CULTURE THAT TEXTS

When God gives a person eternal salvation He will not take it back nor can we lose it. A child of God cannot lose their standing in His sight. God cannot undo what He has put together.

Question 31
Is the Trinity Logically Possible?

Thomas Jefferson, who was the third president of the United States, expressed the sentiment of many outside the church (and some inside the church) when he said that the doctrine of the Trinity is simply too difficult and illogical to believe:

> When we shall have done away with the incomprehensible jargon of the Trinitarian arithmetic, that three are one, and one is three; when we shall have knocked down the artificial scaffolding, reared to mask from view the very simple structure of Jesus; when, in short, we shall have unlearned everything which has been taught since his day, and got back to the pure and simple doctrines he inculcated, we shall then be truly and worthily his disciples.[99]

Many people already struggle to believe in God as a transcendent, all-loving and all-powerful being. The doctrine of the Trinity can amplify these difficulties. The first step is to make sure that our family and friends have a clear understanding of what the term Trinity does and does not mean. The doctrine of the Trinity does not teach that we believe in three gods. The Bible clearly affirms that there is only one God (Deuteronomy 6:4; 1 Corinthians 8:6). However, Christianity teaches that there are personal distinctions within the fundamental unity of God's nature. In other words, within the nature of one God there are three co-eternal, co-equal persons: the Father, the Son, and the Holy Spirit. The three persons share one essence: that of the Almighty God who is the one Creator of the universe.

Obviously, the Christian concept of the Trinity is complex. However, it's important to realize that the early Christian church did not invent the concept of the Trinity in order to dazzle the surrounding world with its intellect and understanding of complex concepts. The church was compelled to embrace the concept of the Trinity for a simple and powerful reason—the testimony of Scripture and the extraordinary

---

[99] Alister E. McGrath, *Understanding the Trinity*, 110.

claims of Jesus of Nazareth. Simply put, the concept of the Trinity is the best explanation for three unquestioned truths that are systematically revealed in Scripture.

- Truth #1: There is only one God (Deuteronomy 6:4; 1 Timothy 2:5).
- Truth #2: Three persons are declared to be deity (1 Corinthians 1:3; John 1:1; John 8:58; Acts 5:4, 5).
- Truth #3: All three persons are simultaneously mentioned as distinct individuals (John 14; Matthew 28:18).

Listen to the following observations by the Christian thinker C.S. Lewis as he expresses his belief that Christians are drawn to this conclusion about the nature of God:

> It is something we could never have guessed, and yet, once we have been told, one almost feels one ought to have been able to guess it because it fits in so well with all the things we know already.[100]
>
> If Christianity was something we were making up, of course we could make it easier. But it is not. We cannot compete, in simplicity, with people who are inventing religions. How could we? We are dealing with Fact. Of course anyone can be simple if he has not facts to bother about.[101]

In his splendid book, *Understanding the Trinity*, Alister McGrath uses the analogy of an iceberg to explain the significance of the Trinity:

> The bit of the iceberg which we notice, which attracts our attention, is its tip. It is the tip of the iceberg which stands out. Some may be tempted to conclude that this is all there is to the iceberg—the bit that we can see. But, as can be shown without too much difficulty, the vast bulk of the iceberg is there to be discovered. . . . The great declaration that "God was reconciling the world to himself in Christ"

---

[100] C.S. Lewis, *The Complete C.S. Lewis Signature Classic*, 134.

[101] C.S. Lewis, *Mere Christianity* (New York: Harper Collins, 2002), 145.

> (2 Corinthians 5:19) turns out to be the tip of the iceberg, and the doctrine of the Trinity the bit which is hidden beneath the surface.[102]

In addition to the three truths that point to the reality of the triune nature of God, the Trinity is implied at various points within the pages of God's Word. When God decided to create the crowning jewel of creation He said, "Let us make man in our image (Genesis 1:26)." In Psalm 110:1 David recognized a clear distinction between the persons "LORD" and "my Lord." Isaiah the prophet predicted that the person born of a virgin would be called Immanuel, which means "God with us (Isaiah 7:14)." In the Great Commission, Jesus commands His disciples to baptize and teach people "in the name of the Father and the Son and the Holy Spirit (Matthew 28:19)." In addition, the benediction of 2 Corinthians 13:1 is a strong affirmation of the equality and unity of Father, Son, and Holy Spirit.

The challenge for Christians is to explain the Trinity in a way that is both logically consistent, as well as historically consistent with our Christian roots. Simply put, the doctrine of the Trinity is not a contradiction. The law of non-contradiction maintains that something cannot be both true and false at the same time and in the same sense. The concept of the Trinity is not the belief that God is three persons and only one person at the same time and in the same sense. Instead, the concept of the Trinity is the belief that there are three persons in one nature. God is one in the sense of His essence but three in the sense of His persons. Since the meanings of "being" and "persons" are different, the doctrine of the Trinity is not a contradiction, just a mystery. When Christians claim that God has one essence and three persons we mean He has one "What" and three "Whos."

It is always going to be extremely difficult to explain the concept of the Trinity to our non-Christian friends. They will scratch their heads, express frustration, and wonder privately why Christians insist on believing things that appear to be irrational. I believe our approach should be much different. We should focus on the message of Christ

---

102 Alister E. McGrath, *Understanding the Trinity*, 112-113.

and realize that His message never would have been possible without God being the way He is. Once again, McGrath brings his insight to bear on this subject:

> When you are explaining what Christianity is all about to your interested friends, you needn't mention the word "Trinity" at all. You speak to them about God, and about the way in which God has revealed himself to us and reconciled us to himself through Jesus Christ. But if you were to sit down and start thinking about the question "What must God be like if he is able to act this way?" you will end up with the doctrine of the Trinity. . . . The proclamation is that God redeems us in Jesus Christ—the doctrine is that God must therefore be a Trinity. It doesn't explain why God is like this, and neither does it pretend to—it simply states that God must be like this if he acts in the way in which Christians know that he does.[103]

TIMELESS TRUTHS FOR A CULTURE THAT TEXTS

The Trinity is not a contradiction—it maintains that God has one essence that is expressed in three distinct persons.

---

[103] Alister E. McGrath, *Understanding the Trinity*, 115.

Question 32
If God is Sovereign, Why Should We Pray?

My good friend Denise has repeatedly struggled with the concept of prayer throughout her journey as a Christian. Denise is a deeply committed believer who is smart and committed to studying the Scriptures. However, Denise has been frustrated at various times when God hasn't responded to very important issues in her life. As a protective device from feeling hurt and disappointed, she often pulls back from the Lord. There are times when she simply won't pray about a crucial area because she doesn't want to be disappointed. Denise is quite aware that God doesn't answer all of our prayers. However, she struggles with the deep tension between the concept of prayer and God's sovereignty.

Many Christians have felt the same way. We have prayed endlessly about a pressing need and God's answer either doesn't come, comes at a wrong time, or we get an entirely different answer than we expected or wanted. Unfortunately, unanswered prayer often forces us to try to figure out why God didn't answer our prayers. Other times, we simply don't pray anymore because we don't think it matters.

C.S. Lewis put his finger on the logical dilemma inherent in the topic of prayer:

> The case against prayer is this: The thing you ask for is either good—for you and for the whole world in general—or else it is not. If it is, then a good and wise God will do it anyway. If it is not, then He won't. In neither case can your prayer make any difference. But if this argument is sound, surely it is an argument not only against praying, but against doing anything whatever?[104]

If we are going to effectively answer these questions, I've found that it can be helpful to remove misconceptions surrounding two questions—what is prayer and what is God's sovereignty?

---

[104] C.S. Lewis, *Work and Prayer*, https://redeeminggod.com/work-and-prayer-by-c-s-lewis/.

WHAT IS PRAYER?

Webster's dictionary defines prayer *as* "a solemn request for help or expression of thanks addressed to God or an object of worship." For the devout believer prayer is a deep conversation with God; the intercourse of the soul with God. Unfortunately, too many believers have been raised with a handful of harmful misconceptions:

- Prayer is a spiritual rabbit's foot that allows us to dictate what God must do.
- Prayer is about twisting God's arm into agreeing with us.
- Prayer is about making deals with God.

Ultimately, prayer is God's pathway to intimacy with Him. It is an intimate act where we connect, confide, and converse with the God of the universe. However, it's vital that we recognize prayer is not fundamentally a means to get what we want from God; prayer is a means God uses to give us what He wants. This is one of the reasons why Jesus emphasized abiding in Him as we engage with God in prayer. In John 15:7 Jesus said, "If you remain in me and my words remain in you, ask whatever you wish, and it will be given you." John Stott, respected author and pastor put it this way, "It is only when Christ's words abide in us that our prayers will be answered. Then we can ask what we will and it shall be done, because we shall will only what He wills."[105]

Obviously, prayer was essential to everything Jesus taught His followers. Jesus commanded His followers to pray (Matthew 6). In fact, He repeatedly taught them parables (Luke 18) that stressed the importance of pleading our case to His Father in prayer. Jesus modeled the importance of prayer throughout His public ministry (Luke 5:16; 9:28). Significantly, Jesus also experienced the perplexing tension between prayer and God's sovereignty as He faced the tension of His will and the will of His Father in the Garden of Gethsemane. It's not

---

[105] W. Bingham Hunter, *The God Who Hears* (Downers Grove: InterVarsity Press, 1986), 195.

difficult to see the legitimate struggle as the Lord uttered the words, "My Father, if it be possible, let this cup pass from me; nevertheless, not as I will, but as you will (Matthew 26:39)." Although Jesus had extreme confidence in God's sovereign control, He still chose to communicate to His Heavenly Father. This would seem like an odd practice and a poor example to believers if there was no sound reason for praying to a sovereign God.

I believe that Jesus understood that prayer was a way God accomplishes aspects of His will. It's not the only thing God uses to accomplish His will but it is one means at His disposal. C.S. Lewis sheds tremendous insight into this issue:

> Infinite wisdom does not need telling what is best, and infinite goodness needs no urging to do it. But neither does God need any of those things that are done by finite agents, whether living or inanimate. He could, if He chose, repair our bodies miraculously without food; or give us food without the aid of farmers, bakers and butchers; or knowledge without the aid of learned men; or convert the heathen without missionaries. Instead, He allows soils and weather and animals and muscles, minds and wills of men to co-operate in the execution of His Will. Pascal said, "God, instituted prayer in order to lend to His creatures the dignity of causality."[106]

Once a person realizes that prayer is something that God uses to accomplish His will, we must think about how we ought to pray. This was illustrated by a story told by famous Soviet dissident, Alexander Solzhenitsyn who described the life of a man named Ivan who endured all the horrors of a Soviet prison camp. One day Ivan was praying with his eyes closed when a fellow prisoner noticed him and said with ridicule, "Prayers won't help you get out of here any faster." Opening his

---

[106] C.S. Lewis, *Essential C.S. Lewis,* edited Lyle W. Dorsett (New York: Touchstone, 1996), 381.

eyes, Ivan answered, "I do not pray to get out of prison but to do the will of God."[107]

Here's what I have recognized over my many years as a follower of Jesus Christ. God doesn't view prayer as purely a recipe for accomplishing His will in the world or to lovingly provide us answers to our requests. God recognizes that prayer is a way to enhance our relationship with Him. When we prioritize prayer in our spiritual journey we discover the following things:

- We grow in our trust and dependence upon the Lord.
- We deepen our friendship with God because we confide in Him completely.
- We learn to appreciate God's power when He responds to our prayers.

I've encouraged my friend Denise to continue to focus on the intimacy and connection that prayer can still bring even when we are confused intellectually about how prayer is consistent with a sovereign God.

WHAT IS GOD'S SOVEREIGNTY?

In the same way that we must be able to properly define prayer, we must also have an accurate and working definition of God's sovereignty. If we don't, it becomes all too easy for us to create problems that are not actually there. Throughout the history of the church, theologians, pastors, and church members have squabbled over the meaning of the concept of God's sovereignty. Although a thorough explanation of God's sovereignty would take many very long chapters, allow me to suggest that looking at this issue through the lens of the Lord Jesus may be a very helpful process.

Jesus affirmed the concepts of human free will (Matthew 23:37) and God's sovereignty (Acts 4:24, 28). Although we will never be able to

[107] Alexander Solzhenitsyn, *A Day in the Life of Ivan Denisovitch* in Mary Love Eyster and Weety Vickery, *Pearls of Wisdom* (Bloomington: WestBow Press, 2014), 44.

perfectly explain that relationship, I believe we should hold these two concepts in perfect balance. There was a crucial and stressful time in Jesus' public ministry when He affirmed the twin truths of God's sovereignty and man's responsibility within one single verse. During the night of his betrayal, He was at the table with His disciples when He uttered these words, "But the hand of him who is going to betray me is with mine on the table. The Son of Man will go as it has been decreed. But woe to that man who betrays him (Luke 22:21-22)."

Jesus recognized that His path to the cross was a part of God's pre-determined plan that He would be crucified for the sins of the world. However, in the same breath, Jesus also pronounced personal judgment (woe) upon Judas for his actions. In other words, Jesus held Judas personally responsible and culpable for his deceptive betrayal. God decreed that the betrayal must happen, but Judas was personally responsible for his act. Of course, personal responsibility is built upon the bedrock truth of human free will. In other words, we are morally responsible for our free actions. John MacArthur puts it this way:

> Every detail of the crucifixion of Christ was under the sovereign control of God and in accord with His eternal purpose. The fact that Judas' betrayal was part of God's plan does not free him from the guilt of a crime he entered into willfully. God's sovereignty is never a legitimate excuse for human guilt.[108]

Within this one single verse Jesus revealed His belief in God's sovereignty and man's responsibility and made no attempt to resolve them. He left these twin truths in tension. Shouldn't we take the same approach? Gifted pastor and author, Timothy Keller expresses a similar insight in his book *Walking with God through Pain and Suffering*:

> The Bible teaches that God is completely in control of what happens in history and yet he exercises that control in such a way that human beings are responsible for their freely chosen actions and the results

---

[108] John MacArthur, *The MacArthur Bible Commentary* (Dallas: Thomas Nelson, 2005), 1326.

> of those actions. Human freedom and God's direction of historical events are therefore completely compatible.[109]

Ultimately, we must embrace both God's sovereignty and man's responsibility knowing that this tension will only be fully resolved in the infinite mind of God. This clearly applies to the Christian's understanding of prayer. The balance between what we ask God to do and what God in His sovereign will chooses to do will always be a struggle. Quite simply, it cannot be resolved within our finite mind.

Ultimately, an antinomy (the apparent contradiction between God's sovereignty and man's free will) can only be fully resolved in the infinite mind of God. It's natural to struggle with this tension in our minds. It's natural to wonder how it does any good. However, it's also natural for us to get on our knees in obedience to our Father and pour out our hearts to Him in prayer. God is eager to connect with all of us who have turned to Him for salvation and comfort during the broken times in our lives.

TIMELESS TRUTHS FOR A CULTURE THAT TEXTS

Prayer will never be fully explained, but our closeness to God in prayer can be fully explored. Prayer is an invitation by God for us to explore the mystery of intimacy with Him—one prayer at a time!

---

[109] Timothy Keller, *Walking with God through Pain and Suffering* (New York: Penguin Group, 2013), 140.

Question 33
Why Are God's Standards of Morality So Different Throughout the Bible?

Many parents take on the roles of "good cop" and "bad cop" in the family. For instance, Dad is the kid's best buddy, and mom is the drill sergeant. Or dad is strict and mom is a sympathizer. One of the difficulties of this approach is that the kids have learned to split their parents. Depending on the situation, kids go to that parent most likely to receive a more favorable response.

Unfortunately, as people read through the Bible it feels like God has adopted the role of "bad cop" in the Old Testament and "good cop" in the New Testament. Think about it! Many times, both the unchurched and the dedicated believer ask simple, yet powerful questions—why is the God of the Old Testament so distinctly different from the God of the New Testament? Why did God command Israel to destroy all the inhabitants of Jericho (Joshua 6), or to annihilate the Canaanites (Deuteronomy 20)? Why is the morality of the Old Testament so very different from the morality of the New Testament? Why has God seemingly changed so much? Old Testament scholar Gleason Archer expresses the perception of many when he says:

> It is commonly thought by those who have not studied the Bible very carefully that the Old Testament presents a God who is full of vengeance and wrath as He enforces the standards of righteousness, whereas the New Testament reveals Him to be full of compassion and love, always seeking to forgive and restore guilty sinners.[110]

There are a handful of principles that might assist us in answering these questions. First, God expresses both love and hate throughout the entire Bible. The New Testament clearly expresses God's love by shining the spotlight on the supreme act of Christ's death on the cross (John 3:16; Romans 8:31-38). However, it may surprise a lot of people that the Old

---

[110] Gleason Archer, *Encyclopedia of Bible Difficulties*, 309.

Testament actually contains more references to God's love. Although some of this is due to the size of the Old Testament (it includes three quarters of the Bible), there is no doubt that God's quality of love is on clear display (Exodus 20:6; Psalm 31:23; Jeremiah 31:3; Hosea 11:1). The Old Testament is full of stories where God extended His mercy to people. Over and over, God patiently waited for His disobedient children to return to Him (Deuteronomy 4:31; Nehemiah 9:31).

It's also important to realize that there is not a clear distinction between a God of wrath in the Old Testament and a God of love in the New Testament. The New Testament clearly reveals God's wrath (John 3:36; Romans 1:18; 2 Thessalonians 1:6-9). In fact, Jesus Himself spoke equally about the realities of heaven (Luke 10:20) and hell (Mark 9:47)—two clear reminders that God is a God of both love and wrath.

Second, God has decided to progressively reveal Himself from the beginning of Scripture (Genesis) to the end of Scripture (Revelation). In other words, God did not reveal all the truth about Himself during the Old Testament. God's revelation of Himself was directly tied to the coming of Christ. This is beautifully expressed with these words:

> In the past God spoke to our ancestors through the prophets at many times and in various ways, but in these last days he has spoken to us by his Son, whom he appointed heir of all things, and through whom also he made the universe.
> Hebrews 1:1-2

God's unquestioned strategy was to reveal Himself progressively to humanity. His revelation would culminate in the God/man. As a result, it shouldn't be a surprise that a higher morality would be revealed at the same time as the ultimate revelation of God's Son, Jesus of Nazareth.

Third, God is an infinitely moral being. As a moral being, God expresses a perfect balance and harmony between His divine wrath and divine love. Divine wrath is not a horrible quality. It is simply God's expression of His inability to tolerate the presence of rebellion, immorality, and disobedience. However, divine wrath can't be seen in isolation from His other attributes. God's wrath and love go hand in hand. Gleason Archer provides his insights:

> The portrait of God is altogether consistent throughout the sixty-six books of the Bible. God's wrath is the reverse side of His love. As the upholder of the moral law—and He would be an unholy, Satan-like God if He failed to uphold it—God must pass judgment and execute sentence on every unrepentant sinner, whether demon or man. The sacrifice of His Son on the cross was the supreme exhibition of God's indignation against sin, for in the hour of final agony even Jesus had to cry out with anguish of soul, "My God, My God, why hast Thou forsaken Me?" And yet the Cross was also the supreme revelation of His unfathomable love, for it was the God-man who suffered there for us, the Just for the unjust, that He might bring us to God.[111]

Finally, God is tremendously patient. Despite the shocking expressions of judgment and wrath in the Old Testament, it's important to interpret these accounts through the lens of history. Listen to the following insight from God's dealing with Abraham, "In the fourth generation your descendants will come back here, for the sin of the Amorites has not yet reached its full measure (Genesis 15:16)." This passage provides us with a unique perspective on the nature of God. The Canaanites had embraced the horrific practice of child sacrifice for over four hundred years. During this period of time, God patiently waited for these people to turn from their sins. He embodied the principle expressed by these words, "maintaining love to thousands, and forgiving wickedness, rebellion and sin. Yet he does not leave the guilty unpunished; he punishes the children and their children for the sin of the parents to the third and fourth generation (Exodus 34:7)."

TIMELESS TRUTHS FOR A CULTURE THAT TEXTS

God did not reveal all the truth about Himself during the Old Testament—He progressively revealed Himself. Although some of the practices in the Old Testament are different, He has always had a perfect balance and harmony between His divine wrath and divine love.

---

[111] Gleason Archer, *Encyclopedia of Bible Difficulties*, 310.

Social/Moral Issues

The modern-day church is in a state of shock regarding the eroding of sexual standards that used to be part of the fabric of America. What is equally surprising is the number of voices within the church who don't hold the same views as their parents about the social issues of our day. Today's younger generation has grown up knowing friends who are from divorced families, who are gay, or debating their own sexuality. This new generation has a much more open view on these social issues. Quite simply, they are tired of the judgmental spirit that seems to come from Christians in regard to a relatively small group of issues. In the face of our culture that embraces same-sex marriage and various sexual orientations, it is increasingly difficult for the younger generation to integrate the faith of their parents into a culture that is almost entirely against their moral worldview.

I am writing these chapters because these topics are discussed on social media and around dinner tables throughout America. I believe the Bible can offer insight in how to approach these issues. However, it's important for me to clearly state my motives and approach. First, I realize that we live within a pluralistic culture. Modern America is comprised of many different faiths, moralities, and viewpoints. I am not trying to set an agenda for the culture of America nor am I insisting that people outside the church embrace the moral standards of the Christian faith. I am simply trying to provide a reasonable explanation for the moral positions as explained by the Bible. Second, although I will focus on certain issues in this section I don't believe God has a special interest in certain sins over other sins. Sin breaks the moral law of God. It's important to realize that there are many sexual sins prevalent inside and outside the church—adultery, lust, divorce, pornography, pedophilia, and child abuse. We should not exclusively focus on one sin to the neglect of others—despite the hot button nature or the emphasis different leaders or pundits place on it. To be honest, God is chiefly concerned with the overall concept of sin and its negative impact on His relationship with humanity. Sin—defined as defiance to the moral law and will of God—is an issue that all of humanity, including Christians, must urgently face. While the issues discussed in these chapters may not directly relate to you, it would be unwise for you to think that there isn't sin in your own life that needs cleansing as well. Christianity offers hope to every single person because a remedy has been provided through the sacrifice of Christ on the cross.

Third, many of the Christian positions on certain moral issues have been routinely interpreted as divisive, non-tolerant, or hateful. All too often, Christians don't act like Jesus when interacting with those of opposite beliefs. Remember, Jesus ate with the tax collectors (Luke 19:1-10) and he reached out to the prostitute (John 4). My intent is not to be divisive or dismissive. I have many friends and associates who have embraced the homosexual/gay lifestyle, believe in same-sex marriage, or believe that abortion is the exclusive right of the mother. While I disagree with their moral standards, I believe they have the right to hold their opinions and I hope my views of what the Bible teaches, will be honored, as well. Further, I believe the church is losing an important moment. We should cultivate friendships and love people unconditionally like Jesus did. At the same time, we can engage in gracious conversations on why we believe a moral line should be drawn at a certain point, while others choose to draw it in a different place. Please read the opinions on the following issues with those sentiments in mind. I trust that every chapter in this section will lead to respectful discussion.

Question 34
Is Morality Relative?

During a meeting of college educators at Harvard University, former Cornell president Frank Rhodes rose to address the issue of reforms by suggesting that it was time for universities to pay real and sustained attention to students' intellectual and moral well-being. Immediately there were gasps, and even catcalls. One indignant student stood to demand of Rhodes, "Who is going to do the instructing? Whose morality are we going to follow?" The audience applauded thunderously, believing that the young man had settled the issue by posing an unanswerable question. Rhodes, who was unable or unwilling to respond, sat down.

My friend Trevor is a businessman who is married with three children. As he and his wife prepare themselves and their children for their teenage years, Trevor is deeply concerned with the moral landscape of our country. In our social media world, his children will be exposed to cultural standards that stand in contrast to the Biblical values he is teaching them. He prepares his kids with numerous practical and helpful ideas for when they dialogue with people outside the faith. He reminds them that the real danger of people not believing in God is not that they will believe nothing, but that they will believe in anything. He also helps his children reason with their friends by reminding them that everyone draws a moral line in the sand—the question is where do you draw it and why do you draw it?

Every day we are reminded of the appeal of ethical relativism in the post-modern world. Everywhere we turn we hear objections that have been repeated so often without refutation that they have become part of our cultural fabric:

- "That's true for you, but not for me."
- "So many people disagree—relativism must be true."
- "Why are you imposing your morality on me?"
- "Who are you to judge others?"

We can't sit by idly and allow people to suggest that all morality is relative. Like my friend Trevor, we must have a basic strategy that helps people to see that the universe was brought into existence by our moral Creator who will ultimately ask us to give account of our lives to Him. In his helpful book *Relativism: Feet Firmly Planted in Mid-Air,* Greg Koukl, who is one of the great experts on relativism, suggests several basic flaws that are very helpful when talking to people within our culture. I've provided a summation of what he has to say in a handful of them below:

FLAW #1: IF MORALITY IS RELATIVE; NOTHING IS WRONG.

Moral relativists cannot claim that everything is relative and at the same time find something immoral. Here's the reality—no one actually believes that. Although we live in a very diverse world there are very clear universal truths that even the most casual observer must admit exist. Murder, rape, and torturing babies are always wrong. We live within a culture that still shows moral outrage when confronted with morally heinous acts. We still feel the violation of innocence that occurred because of the school shootings in Sandy Hook, the shootings at a church in Charleston, or the executions of police officers in Dallas.

FLAW # 2: IF MORALITY RELATIVE; WHY WORRY ABOUT EVIL?

If there are really no moral absolutes, how can a person complain about evil? Wickedness is a moral judgement of something that falls short of an objective moral standard. The presence of evil in the world reminds us that we live in a universe that was created by a moral God. In the aftermath of the Sandy Hook killings, Governor Daniel Malloy said, "Evil visited this community today." There was a standard that was violated on that day. Moral relativism fails to recognize that evil violates an objective moral standard that most people embrace.

FLAW # 3: IF MORALITY IS RELATIVE; WHY BLAME OR PRAISE ANYONE?

If there is nothing good or bad, then it is difficult to praise or blame anyone. We praise people like Mother Theresa for doing morally good things. We revile people like Adolf Hitler, Osama Bin Laden or ISIS. Praising or blaming another person is the equivalent of making a moral judgment. This moral judgment is based upon our knowledge of a moral standard of what is right or wrong. The concept of justice is tied to some kind of moral standard. There is no meaning to justice without morality.

FLAW # 4: IF MORALITY IS RELATIVE; WHY BE TOLERANT?

Supporters of the notion of tolerance claim that everyone is under the moral obligation to accept and not interfere with the opinions and behaviors of those who disagree with us. The problem with this is that it seems that tolerance itself is a moral absolute—something that moral relativism rejects. In addition, most moral relativists practice selective tolerance especially as it relates to those who hold to moral absolutes.

It's important to remind ourselves that we can help people see the failure of moral relativism by using everyday stories and pictures from life. Here are a couple of examples.

First, everyone has some person in history that they applaud as a moral hero. For example, if you've ever seen *The Killing Fields* or *Schindler's List* you recognize that the lead characters (based upon actual history) were moral heroes. They stood up against brutal injustice within a culture. They took a stand and said, "This is morally wrong and that is morally right". You can't applaud those movies as stirring tributes of the nobility of man without asserting that we live in a moral culture derived from a moral creator.

Second, if a person suggests that you have no right to tell people that what they do is right or wrong, you can say, "Would you give me your laptop or iPhone? I know you'll miss them but I'm not doing anything wrong. It's just something that I feel like doing." Practically speaking, moral relativism doesn't work. The moment that you do something or suggest something that from their vantage point is wrong, they will claim that what you are doing is wrong.

TIMELESS TRUTHS FOR A CULTURE THAT TEXTS

Moral absolutes are a fact of our world. Although we live in a very diverse world, there are very clear universal truths—murder, rape, and torture of babies are clearly wrong.

Question 35
Does the Bible Teach that Homosexual Behavior is Wrong?

Over the past ten years, public opinion about homosexuality has continued to shift away from a historical Judeo-Christian understanding. The Pew Research Center's 2013 Global Attitudes survey asked 40,117 respondents in 40 countries about various moral issues. The poll indicated that the public is divided over whether engaging in homosexual behavior is a sin: 45% say it is a sin while an identical percentage says it is not. However, it's clear that societies' views have shifted because in 2003, a majority (55%) viewed homosexual behavior as sinful, while 33% disagreed.

As our culture continues to embrace homosexuality, many people within the walls of the church will be asked to interact and respond to family and friends who are homosexual. I think of my friend Taylor who has had to deal with the reality of homosexuality in a very personal way. Taylor is in his late 40's and is married with children. Taylor has always embraced the Biblical position which teaches that homosexual behavior, like all sexual intimacy outside of marriage, is wrong. However, one of Taylor's children recently expressed her solidarity with the gay/lesbian lifestyle. How should a Christian parent respond? How should they process all the teachings in Scripture and the various related questions such as, are people born gay or is same-sex marriage wrong?

Taylor's conviction toward the Biblical teaching has not changed. However, his attitude has changed dramatically. Taylor used to be very dogmatic and cold-hearted because he felt he had to protect the moral convictions of God's Word. However, his approach has changed. He's still committed to the Biblical truth but now he wants to hear the views of his lesbian daughter. He wants to understand the thinking and the rationale of those committed to this lifestyle—he wants to understand so that he can better connect to others and better connect to the daughter he loves.

As I've listen to Taylor's personal journey I've sensed the importance of two principles. First, unconditional love for a person is not the same as unconditional approval for a person's lifestyle. God has not only demonstrated unconditional love to all of humanity, He has asked us to love people regardless of their choices. It's vital to recognize that a person's choices in the sexual arena does not fundamentally define a person. Every person in the world is made in the image of God and is therefore entitled to be loved as God loves.

Second, it is absolutely necessary for Christians to consistently embrace the moral standards expressed within the Bible. The Scriptures don't simply focus on homosexual behavior; they consistently teach the principle that God is against all extra-marital sexual behavior. All too often we seem to think that homosexual behavior is worse than other sins. The church must not pick and choose which extra-marital behavior they deem most offensive.

In contrast to the prevailing opinions of our culture, the Biblical position on homosexual behavior is quite clear. Although some mainline denominations and homosexual churches provide alternative interpretations of the traditional Scriptural teaching, these are not consistent with a clear and consistent interpretation of the Bible.

Throughout the Old and New Testaments, the Biblical authors repeatedly stress the prohibition of homosexuality behavior. Genesis 2:18-24 expresses God's divine intention for the human family—it is limited to the heterosexual union between man and woman in marriage. Genesis 19:14-19 describes the destruction of Sodom for their wickedness, which included the rampant homosexuality in the city. Leviticus 18 and 20 provides a long list of morally reprehensible behaviors, in which homosexuality is included.

The male-female union is the only model of sexual behavior consistently praised in both the Old and New Testaments. Although other forms of behavior—polygamy and the use of concubines—were an accepted practice in the Old Testament, a monogamous relationship between husband and wife is the standard upheld as the Scriptural ideal. Although Jesus never specifically addressed the issue of homosexuality he clearly addressed God's divine intent for human sexuality when he stated, "From the beginning of the creation God made them male and female." In his response to a question about divorce, Jesus emphasized "one flesh" sexual union between a male and a female and a total monogamous relationship.

The New Testament continues the clear prohibition against homosexual behavior with Paul's central teaching in Romans 1:24-27. In this passage, the Apostle Paul attempts to lay a foundation for God's universal judgment of mankind in light of those who have rejected God despite His revelation through creation (Romans 1:18-20), conscience (Romans 2:15), and providence (Acts 14:15-17). As a result of this disobedience, "God gave them over in the lusts of their hearts to impurity. . . . God gave them over to degrading passions; for their women exchanged the natural function . . . The men abandoned the natural function (Romans 1:24, 26, 27)."

The implication from Romans seems to identify homosexual behavior as one of the consequences of the fall of humanity. Noted ethical expert Scott Rae describes it this way, "instead of responding to our innate tendency toward opposite sex attraction, but because of sin, the human race developed the potential for homosexuality. This potential is often realized when certain development factors are present."[112]

The church's moral concern should not be focused exclusively on a person's homosexual orientation. To be honest, the Bible does not specifically address the issue of homosexual orientation. However, what seems clear throughout the Bible is its injunction against homosexuality actions. In other words, the moral issue is what a person does with this homosexual orientation toward a person of the same-sex. Whether the issue is heterosexual attraction or homosexual attraction, the primary focus of the Bible is directed toward a person's immoral thoughts and actions (Matthew 5:28).

We should not condemn an individual for their sexual identity—rather we caution followers of Christ to avoid sexual promiscuity before marriage or a person's violation of the one-flesh relationship once a person is

---

[112] Scott B. Rae, *Moral Choices: An Introduction to Ethics*, (Grand Rapids: Zondervan, 2009), 282.

married. I think the same approach should be applied to those who struggle with homosexual impulses. Noted Christian ethical expert, Scott Rae follows these guidelines with this piece of advice:

> The options for the Christian homosexual would be the same as for the Christian heterosexual—either abstinence or heterosexual sex in marriage. Some Christians who struggle with their sexual identity have grasped this distinction and are attempting to be faithful to Christ and sexually pure at the same time.[113]

TIMELESS TRUTHS FOR A CULTURE THAT TEXTS

God has asked the Christian to be uncompromising in our convictions and unconditional in our love. There is no other option!

[113] Ibid., 283.

Question 36
Are People Born Homosexual/Gay?

For the first time, a majority of Americans say that homosexuals are born that way. According to the latest Gallup poll in 2015, 51 percent of Americans say that people are born gay or lesbian, while only 30 percent say outside factors such as upbringing and environment determine sexual orientation.

The popular sentiment that a person is born gay is very powerful because it resonates with the public's perception that a person can't be held responsible for a trait or orientation that they were given at birth. In most people's eyes, it's not fair. Although this an emotionally charged issue, I think it is important to lay out some observations that may allow folks to have a constructive conversation with people who have a different viewpoint.

In 1991, psychologist Michael Bailey of Northwestern University and psychiatrist Richard Pillard of Boston University School of Medicine compared sets of identical male twins to fraternal twins (genetic ties are not as close). They were hoping to determine if homosexuality might be a genetically inherited trait. Their research indicated a high incidence of homosexuality among the identical twins as compared to the fraternal and non-twin brothers. Their work was cited with great fanfare in a Newsweek article entitled, "Is This Child Gay?"

Despite the headlines, it's important to point out that if people are genetically homosexuals so that they have no choice but to be gay, you would expect that identical twins would have a 100% correspondence in either both being heterosexual or both being homosexual. However, numerous studies on identical twins show that the discordant rate (lack of harmony) between identical twins is between 48% and 52%. In other words, roughly half of the twins were both homosexual and half were composed of one homosexual and one heterosexual.

Jeffrey Satinover is an Orthodox Jew who obtained a Master of Education degree in Clinical Psychology and Public Practice from Harvard University. He makes the following observation:

> If "homosexuality is genetic," as activists and their media supporters repeatedly claim, the concordance rate between identical twins—that is, the incidence of the two twins either both being homosexual or both being heterosexual—will be 100%. There would never be a discordant pair—a pair with one homosexual twin and one heterosexual twin. When we say that "eye color is genetically determined," this is what we mean. That's why identical twins always have the same eye color. If we were to find genuinely identical twins with different eye colors we would be forced to conclude that although genetics may exert an influence on eye color, it does not determine it. Eye color would be dependent upon some additional factor as well.[114]

Famous Lesbian author Dr. Camille Paglia is quite blunt in her admissions:

> Homosexuality is not normal. . . . Procreation is the single relentless rule. That is the norm. Our sexual bodies were designed for reproduction. . . . No one is born gay. The idea is ridiculous. . . . Homosexuality is an adaption, not an inborn trait.[115]

Obviously, we don't have a complete understanding of the exact causative factors that lead to a person's homosexuality. Research clearly tells us that there are a number of unique experiences that seem to be present in someone with a homosexual orientation. However, it's also clear that not all these factors apply to everyone. Therefore, it seems prudent to assume that each individual who experiences same-sex attraction will have a unique set of experiences and factors that contribute in different ways to their sexual identity. Columbia University professors Richard Friedman and Jennifer Downey summarize the evidence/research:

---

[114] Jeffrey Satinover, *Homosexuality and the Politics of Truth* (Grand Rapids: Baker Book House), 83.

[115] Glenn T. Stanton and Bill Maier, *Marriage on Trial: The Case Against Same-Sex Marriage and Parenting* (Downers Grove: InterVarsity Press, 2004), 138.

> At clinical conferences one often hears that homosexual orientation is fixed and unmodifiable. Neither assertion is true. . . . The assertion that homosexuality is genetic . . . must be dismissed out of hand as a general principle of psychology. . . . What causes homosexuality? It is apparent that biological, psychological and social factors interacting in complex and various ways shape human sexual orientation.[116]

Here are a handful of factors that both secular and Christian psychologists and researchers have recognized play a role in determining sexual orientation:

SEXUAL ORIENTATION IS INFLUENCED BY GENETIC PREDISPOSITION

Scientific research for human behavior is at an all-time high. There is an insatiable desire to determine why people make the choices that they do. Although we are intrigued by the various research and the tremendous complexity of human beings, we must avoid two simplistic extremes. First, we can't ignore the role that genetics play within our lives. The more we observe from scientific studies, the more we must acknowledge the complex intermingling of genetics and our surrounding environment. Second, we must never minimize human choice. The essence of humanity is not simply a complex series of physical hard wiring in our brain that compels us to act without a choice. If this were the case, the entire notion of free choice would disappear. Clearly, we hold people responsible for all kinds of behavior even if they had some kind of predisposition or inherent susceptibility to certain behaviors or vices.

SEXUAL ORIENTATION CAN BE SHAPED BY FAMILY DYSFUNCTION

Irving Bieber and his colleagues found a triangular pattern in the family backgrounds of many male homosexuals. In his book entitled *Homosexuality: A Psychoanalytic Study of Male Homosexuals*, they

---

[116] Glenn T. Stanton and Bill Maier, *Marriage on Trial: The Case Against Same-Sex Marriage and Parenting*, 137-138.

compared 106 male homosexuals with 100 male heterosexuals. They observed, "Mothers of homosexuals were reported to have enmeshed, seductive relationships with their sons, while fathers were more commonly reported to be distant, detached or rejecting."[117] At the most basic level, the idea is that male homosexuality is caused by the failure of normal development of a secure male identity."[118] This theory is drawn from a normal understanding of when a child bonds with a deeply loved father and is encouraged and supported by a loving mother. Early childhood experiences may influence one person in a greater way due to biological contributors and the nature and nurture of one's childhood. In other words, they provide a push in the direction of homosexuality, though no one experience causes a person to be homosexual.

SEXUAL ORIENTATION IS INFLUENCED BY CULTURAL STANDARDS

Cultural standards are one of the most powerful forces in human history. Standards either encourage people to embrace virtue or provide permission for people to pursue vice. In a positive sense, culture has the capacity to pressure people to avoid certain behavior whether it is the danger of smoking, texting while driving, or racial bigotry. Unfortunately, our culture has the capacity to influence people by suggesting that a certain behavior is normal or embraced by the culture. Many young people have been influenced to take illicit drugs, embrace sexual promiscuity, or to consider suicide. Jeffrey Satinover suggests the influence of cultural standards in the development of a homosexual orientation:

> Given that such cultures have existed where the incidence of homosexuality is far greater than at present, the incidence of homosexuality is clearly influenced by mores. Where people endorse and encourage homosexuality, the incidence increases;

---

[117] Stanton L. Jones and Mark A. Yarhouse, *Homosexuality: The Use of Scientific Research in the Church's Moral Debate* (Downer's Grove: InterVarsity, 2000), 54.

[118] Stanton L. Jones and Mark A. Yarhouse, *Homosexuality: The Use of Scientific Research in the Church's Moral Debate*, 54.

> where they reject it, it decreases. These factors have nothing to do with its genetics.[119]

SEXUAL ORIENTATION CAN BE INFLUENCED BY CHILDHOOD SEXUAL TRAUMA

Childhood sexual trauma has been considered a factor in the origins of same-sex attraction. In one of the more comprehensive studies of human sexuality in America (*The Social Organization of Sexuality: Sexual Practices in the United States)*, Edward Laumann and his team found that a child's experience of sexual abuse more than tripled the likelihood of later reporting homosexual orientation. Of course, it may be possible that these kinds of childhood activities may also be "reinforcing same-sex feelings that were already present."[120]

However, a fair-minded Christian must acknowledge the following:

> That childhood sexual trauma or sexual activity in childhood or early sexual debut does not directly "cause" homosexuality or experiences of same-sex attraction. If they did, then all, not just some, of the individuals who went through such experiences would turn out homosexual. Same-sex childhood experience may leave a child who also has a secure identification with the same-sex parent basically unaffected. . . . This research does not support the idea of one-to-one correlation.[121]

SEXUAL ORIENTATION IS INFLUENCED BY HUMAN CHOICE

Human choice is one of the factors that influences the continued development of a person's sexual orientation. Sexual orientation is assumed to be shaped and reshaped by a cascade of choices made in the context of changing circumstances in one's life and by enormous

---

[119] Jeffrey Satinover, 116.

[120] Ibid, 58.

[121] Stanton L. Jones and Mark A. Yarhouse, *Homosexuality: The Use of Scientific Research in the Church's Moral Debate,* 58.

social and cultural pressures. Once again, Jones and Yarhouse suggest the following as personality traits of the homosexual person:

> Perhaps they have the types of temperaments that make it more difficult to fully identify as a typical man or woman. Perhaps they crave the forbidden or exotic. Perhaps they experience sexual arousal to a wider array of stimuli. Perhaps they have the physical appearance that makes them attractive to same-sex partners. . . . They may very well identify or experience themselves as gay or lesbian.[122]

If biology is the sole determiner of morality, how can society hold people responsible for their actions? What about the alcoholic? What about the violent aggressor? What happens to our culture if an inborn genetic inclination toward violent activities is discovered? What if we discover genetic inclinations toward murder, child abuse, spousal abuse, violence, or drug addiction? Will this excuse the corresponding behavior? Does it remove personal responsibility? Of course, not; this would be morally absurd.

Since we do not yet have a complete understanding of the exact causative factors that lead to a person's homosexuality, and since it appears that people possess certain factors but not every factor, it seems prudent to assume that each individual who experiences same-sex attraction will have a unique set of experiences and factors that contribute in different ways to their sexual identity.

Regardless of the predisposition that people might possess (alcoholism, abuse, or homosexuality) everyone is still morally culpable for their actions. Jones and Yarhouse describe it powerfully:

> Homosexual persons are not subhuman robots whose acts are predetermined. They are moral agents who inherit tendencies from biology and environment, and who share in shaping their character by the responses they make to their life situations. Like all persons,

---

[122] Jones and Yarhouse, 83.

they must ask, "This is what I want to do, but is it what I should do?" The existence of inclinations or predispositions does not erase the need for moral evaluation of those inclinations.[123]

TIMELESS TRUTHS FOR A CULTURE THAT TEXTS

Many factors might pre-dispose someone to the homosexual/gay lifestyle but they do not pre-determine it. If it did, we would lose the dignity of free will.

[123] Ibid., 90.

Question 37
Is Same-Sex Marriage Wrong?

In one of the many clear evidences that Christian morality is being jettisoned or challenged by contemporary American culture, a recent Pew Center Research Poll revealed powerful trends on the issue of same-sex marriage. In Pew Research polling in 2001, Americans opposed same-sex marriage by a 57% to 35% margin. Since then, support for same-sex marriage has grown steadily. Today, a majority of Americans support same-sex marriage (54%), compared with 39% who oppose it.[124]

It seems more and more clear that same-sex marriage will continue to be legalized throughout the 50 states and continue to be viewed as socially acceptable by a growing segment of the population. Of course, the issue of same-sex marriage in the United States has followed a legal roller-coaster journey. In 1996, the overwhelming majority of both houses of Congress passed the Defense of Marriage Act (DOMA). Only 81 out of 535 (House & Senate) members voted against this brief statement affirming the historic definition of marriage. In particular, section 3 of DOMA provided a definition of marriage which read as follows:

> In determining the meaning of any Act of Congress, or of any ruling, regulation, or interpretation of the various administrative bureaus and agencies of the United States, the word "marriage" means only a legal union between one man and one woman as husband and wife, and the word "spouse" refers only to a person of the opposite sex who is a husband or a wife.[125]

Over the course of less than 20 years, the legal climate over the issue of same-sex marriage has changed dramatically. In 2013, DOMA was

---

124 Pew Research Center, March 2014 "Changing Attitudes on Gay Marriage" http://www.pewforum.org/2015/07/29/graphics-slideshow-changing-attitudes-on-gay-marriage

125 http://en.wikipedia.org/wiki/Defense_of_Marriage_Act.

overturned by a 5-to-4 majority of the Supreme Court (*United States v. Windsor*). The Supreme Court's position overturned a law that denied federal benefits to same-sex couples. The decision did not guarantee a right to same-sex marriage, but it allowed people who live in states that allow same-sex marriage to receive the same federal benefits as heterosexual couples. In the majority opinion of the court written by Justice Anthony Kennedy, the following argument was stated:

> This requires the Court to hold, as it now does, that DOMA is unconstitutional as a deprivation of the liberty of the person protected by the Fifth Amendment of the Constitution. The liberty protected by the Fifth Amendment's Due Process Clause contains within it the prohibition against denying to any person the equal protection of the laws. . . . DOMA singles out a class of persons deemed by a State entitled to recognition and protection to enhance their own liberty. It imposes a disability on the class by refusing to acknowledge a status the State finds to be dignified and proper. DOMA instructs all federal officials, and indeed all persons with whom same-sex couples interact, including their own children, that their marriage is less worthy than the marriages of others.[126]

Obergefell v. Hodges 2015 is the most recent case that has changed the legal landscape in relationship to same-sex marriage. The United States Supreme Court held in a 5–4 decision that the fundamental right to marry is guaranteed to same-sex couples by both the due process clause and the equal protection clause of the Fourteenth Amendment of the United States Constitution. Obergefell v. Hodges required all states to issue marriage licenses to same-sex couples and to recognize same-sex marriages validly performed in other jurisdictions.

As in so many areas of the Christian's interaction with secular culture, most Christians seem ill-equipped to respond to the effective talking points on same-sex marriage. The compassionate pleas by our

---

[126] http://www.nytimes.com/interactive/2013/06/26/us/annotated-supreme-court-decision-on-doma.

neighbors, family, and friends are regularly re-enforced by the media, movie stars, and politicians. These responses have become so ingrained into people's subconscious that people rarely hear an effective or compelling response by an informed and compassionate Christian.

Here are a handful of reasons why Christians have serious concerns about the trend toward embracing same-sex marriage.

REASON #1: MALE-FEMALE MARRIAGE HAS BEEN THE IDEAL THROUGHOUT HUMAN HISTORY

Our culture is undergoing one of the most radical social experiments ever proposed in our nation—the redefinition of the institution of marriage. For a true perspective on this issue it's important to remember the following:

> Up until the last few "milliseconds" of human history, no society anywhere in the world, at any time in recorded history, has ever affirmed homosexual marriage. Until very recent history, homosexual unions have never officially been considered a normal, morally equal part of any culture.[127]

While a few societies have practiced polygamy, the core of the family has always consisted of men and women raising the next generation in a cooperative way. And marriage is not just a Christian institution. Every one of the major world religions upholds and honors marriage between a man and a woman.

From a purely evolutionary viewpoint (survival of the fittest), homosexuality cannot be the norm for society since a full embracing of homosexuality (apart from the modern medical world) would not be able to account for the survival of the species. Everyone enters humanity through the gate of heterosexuality, with the union of the male sperm and female egg being the mandatory portal. Homosexuality can never

---

[127] Bill Maier in Joe Dallas and Nancy Heche, *The Complete Christian Guide to Understanding Homosexuality*, 349-350.

produce the next generation. This is why no society has ever recognized it as the primary form of family.

Despite these observations from history, the issue of same-sex marriage will not go away because in a world where all cultures, religions, and nations are viewed as equal—the recognition of the equality of same-sex marriage to the male-female ideal is seen as essential. Although rights might have been given to same-sex couples without the redefinition of marriage, the symbolism of equality in marriage will continue to be the prize of many within our culture.

We've all heard stories of gays who have been denied basic rights associated with marriage. Those of us who oppose the moral foundation of same-sex marriage must recognize the human price that many gay couples have experienced as these issues are debated in the public square. However, although the rally cry of "fairness" is constantly heard by supporters of same-sex marriage, it's equally important to ask whether or not it is fair to society to establish this social policy. Although it sounds intolerant to many in our culture, the male-female marriage has been the ideal/standard in every civilization throughout history.

Tragically, the moment our society claims a constitutional right to provide marriage on an equal basis then we open up the door to polygamous relationships, sibling relationships, adult/child relationships, or parent/adult relationships. What moral standard could be used to prevent these relationships or other alternative relationships from claiming the rights and privileges of marriage? Many proponents of same-sex relationships claim that as long as two people love each other they should be able to get married. People in any alternative relationship could make this same claim. People might even attempt to claim that incestuous or polygamous relationships should no longer be view as illegal in America—opening yet another door to redefine marriage.

REASON #2: SAME-SEX MARRIAGE IS NOT THE SAME AS INTER-RACIAL MARRIAGE

Thirty years ago, interracial marriage was illegal in some states but the courts ruled that these laws were unconstitutional. Many within the gay/lesbian lifestyle view same-sex marriage in the same way. They believe the same principle is at stake—the freedom to marry—the freedom to love the person they wish.

There is no legitimate comparison between race and gender. Gender is the great divide between humanity—male and female. People understand that there is a fundamental difference between men and women. We separate sporting events, clothing, public restrooms, and sometimes schools based upon gender. None of these actions are immoral. However, we no longer have separate restrooms for blacks and restrooms for all other races because that is immoral. In an enlightened society, the color of a person's skin does not fundamentally change what we have in common—our humanity. To suggest there is a fundamental difference based upon skin color is racist. Simply put, opposing interracial marriage was wrong and is wrong, but it's not equivalent to same-sex marriage. Noted conservative talk show host, Dennis Prager makes this observation:

> If opposition to same-sex marriage is as immoral as racism, why did not great moral thinkers, in all of history, ever advocate male-male or female-female marriage? Opposition to racism was advocated by every great moral thinker. Moses, for example, married a black woman. . . .the equality of human beings of every race was a central tenet of Judaism, Christianity, Islam, and other world religions. But no one—not Moses, Jesus, Buddha, Muhammad, Aquinas, Gandhi, not the Bible or the Koran or any other sacred text, nor even a single anti-religious secular thinker of the Enlightenment—ever advocated redefining marriage to include members of the same sex.[128]

Same-sex couples have a right to be together but they don't have a right to categorically redefine the institution of marriage—which every society and every religion in history has embraced.

---

[128] Dennis Prager *"Why a Good Person Can Vote Against Same-Sex Marriage"* Tuesday, October 30, 2012, http://www.dennisprager.com/why-a-good-person-can-vote-against-same-sex-marriage.

REASON #3: OPPOSITION TO SAME-SEX MARRIAGE IS NOT HATEFUL OR BIGOTED

It's important to make the distinction that we are not saying that heterosexuals are superior to homosexuals just like we wouldn't say that a married person is superior to a single person. In fact, the homosexual and heterosexual are equal in God's eyes. We have all been created in God's image. Despite the equality of every single person, society has a right to prefer that the building block of society should be based upon a married mother and father.

There is nothing inherently hateful or bigoted about drawing a line in regard to sexual conduct. It's important to remember that consensual sex between adults is not always acceptable. Father-daughter or brother-sister sexual relations are morally wrong. Why should people who believe the line should be drawn at homosexual sex be viewed as more bigoted that those who draw the line at incestuous sex? There is clearly nothing wrong with modern society resisting the kind of man-boy sex that was rampant in Ancient Greece. In other words, merely drawing the moral line in a different place than other people in our culture does not make us hateful or bigoted.

REASON #4: SAME-SEX MARRIAGE WILL LEAD TO THE LIMITS OF RELIGIOUS EXPRESSION

The First Amendment guarantees each citizen's religious liberty, which includes the right to voice our opinions in the public square. However, increasingly we witness more and more criticism and hostility toward religious institutions for their moral stands on homosexuality and same-sex marriage. Although proponents of same-sex marriage attempt to assure the religious community that our rights to free speech will not be hindered, there is substantial evidence to the contrary. eHarmony, the country's largest online dating service was sued for only matching men and women. The suit claimed that it violated anti-discrimination laws and was forced to begin a same-sex online service. In 2014, Houston mayor, Annise Parker, the city's first openly lesbian mayor, issued subpoenas that demanded the sermons of pastors who may have spoken on the topic of homosexuality or gender identity. This was clearly an attempt to limit the religious viewpoints of those within the church whose opinions on these issues differ than the LGBT community. In a culture that opposes anything that advocates moral absolutes or exclusive truth, the focus in the future will be on the church's moral views.

REASON #5: SAME-SEX MARRIAGE IS NOT IDEAL FOR CHILDREN

Civilization has nurtured children for over a millennia based upon the belief that a child learns something essential when reared in a household that includes both sexes. Proponents of same-sex marriage can't argue that mothers or fathers are useless so they must claim that having a mother and father are no better for children than two same-sex parents.

Does anyone actually think that a child is better off without a mother and father? Death, divorce, abandonment, or single parent's mistakes can easily deprive a child of a mother or father. However, only same-sex marriage would legally ensure that children are deprived from birth of either a mother or father. The history of humanity has demonstrated that male and female parents make distinctive contributions to the well-being of a child.

Same-sex proponents claim that studies show there is no difference whether the parents are same sex or male and female. However, Professor Don Browning of the University of Chicago disagreed when he wrote in the New York Times, "We know next to nothing" about the effects of same-sex parenting on children. In addition, he states, "The body of sociological knowledge about same-sex parenting is scant at best. . . . There are no rigorous, large-scale studies on the effect of same-sex marriage on the couple's children."[129]

We are not trying to say that there aren't loving and devoted same-sex parents who wish the very best for their children. It's simply important to recognize that children of same-sex couples face some inherent

---

[129] Dennis Prager, *Same Sex Marriage: Good for Gays; Bad for Children*, http://www.dennisprager.com/same-sex-marriage-good-for-gays-bad-for-children/

difficulties. Judith Stacey and Timothy Biblarz (both supporters of same-sex marriage) conducted a comprehensive review of the same-sex parenting literature and published their results in the journal *American Sociological Review.* In it, they noted significant differences in children raised by gay couples:

- They are more likely to engage in behavior that is non-normative for their gender—little boys aren't really sure what it means to be male, and the little girls aren't really sure what it means to be female.
- The girls are more likely to be promiscuous.
- Both the boys and the girls are more likely to experiment with homosexual behavior. That doesn't mean they will ultimately self-identify as gay adults, but it does mean they are more likely to "give it a try"—to experiment with same-sex relationships as teens and young adults.[130]

No one is saying that same-sex couples can't be caring. We aren't saying our family and friends can't be nice people or good citizens. We aren't saying they can't form loving relationships. We aren't even saying that there are not nurturing, caring gay couples that are committed to raising children. However, we are trying to remind our culture of the importance of pursuing the ideal. Famous Chicago Pastor, Erwin Lutzer describes the opportunity this way:

> God intended that every child have a mother and a father who are an example of commitment, caring, and love. Not only is such a child given a sense of security, but he or she also sees femininity and masculinity modeled in a complementary relationship. Of course, in our world with rampant divorce, immorality, and the redefinition of the family, this ideal is becoming a memory. However—and this is important—we must work toward the ideal even though we know we shall not achieve it, rather than work against it, defying the Designer who made us all.[131]

---

[130] Bill Maier in Dallas and Heche, 358.

[131] Erwin W. Lutzer, *The Truth About Same-Sex Marriage*, 75.

Ultimately, we are saying that same-sex marriage distorts the fundamental view of marriage that has been universally accepted throughout the history of mankind. In other words, we are part of a social experiment in redefining marriage that is absolutely new within human history. Unfortunately, the church has reserved some of its fiercest moral condemnation for the gay community. We must realize that God is opposed to all sin—whether it is present in our lives or the lives of others. All too often we have ignored our favorite heterosexual sins (adultery, fornication, divorce, and pornography) and focused hate and derision toward those who embrace a homosexual lifestyle. Everyone stands equally flawed in the presence of a perfect God and everyone stands equally forgiven at the foot of the cross. Although we disagree with the moral standards embraced by many within our culture, we must embrace fellow sinners with unconditional love.

TIMELESS TRUTHS FOR A CULTURE THAT TEXTS

The family is the backbone of every culture—it is the fabric by which young lives are developed. Let's not experiment with the next generation without pausing to ask "says who?"

Question 38
Is Abortion Immoral?

"Abortion: Stories Women Tell" is HBO's latest advocacy-oriented documentary (2016), chronicling the impact of Missouri abortion restrictions (72-hour waiting period) on those forced to cross the Illinois border to seek procedures. The 93-minute film unfolds from the perspectives of multiple women—those who are seeking abortions as well as activists on both sides of the issue. The film focuses on Amie, a 30-year-old single mother who works 70 to 90 hours per week. "I cannot put my family through another kid right now," she says, before driving more than two hours into Illinois.

The stories behind this documentary are a stark reminder that although *Roe v. Wade* legalized abortion, people have not forgotten the date January 20, 1973. For many people it was the day when religion and government stepped out of the private lives of women. For other people it marked the moment when our government sanctioned the attack on the unborn. In the landmark decision of *Roe v. Wade* (1973) the Supreme Court drew the lines that have divided people in America ever since.

In discussing the issue of abortion several things must clearly be kept in mind. First, my intent is not to retry this issue in the Supreme Court. It seems to me that for the foreseeable future that *Roe v. Wade* will continue to be the law of the land as it has been for the last forty years. However, although the legality of abortion seems unassailable for the near future, the morality of abortion must continue to be debated in the court of public opinion. Second, I am also not interested in demonizing or traumatizing women who have made the choice of abortion in the past or are presently wrestling with the issue. A woman is not fundamentally defined by her choices over an unwanted child. Everyone, even the unborn child, has been made in the image of God and deserves to be loved and respected despite one's choices.

Roe v. Wade ruled that a woman has a constitutional right to an abortion, but that the state also has an interest in protecting the health of a woman and the potential life of a fetus. Following the medical field's division of a woman's pregnancy into three trimesters, the government determined that during the first trimester, a woman has the unquestioned right to abortion on demand. After the first trimester, the state was required to place some limits upon the demands of abortion. For example, after viability (the moment a fetus can live outside the mother), the state was required to protect the potential life of the fetus by regulated and prohibited abortion except in the case of preserving the life or health of the mother. *Planned Parenthood v. Casey* (1992) provided the high court with the opportunity to overturn *Roe v. Wade*. However, the Supreme Court reasoned that the right to abortion was consistent with the right to privacy. The Supreme Court justices further argued that abortion rights are consistent with the ideas of both personal autonomy and bodily integrity.

These and other Supreme Court decisions have made it quite clear that abortion on demand will continue to be legal in the United States for the foreseeable future. With no legal avenue available for opponents of abortion, the only available option is to use intellectual and moral persuasion to win the hearts and minds of the American public. The next portion of this chapter will focus on interacting with a few of the most central arguments for the pro-choice position.

ARGUMENT #1: A WOMAN HAS CONTROL OVER HER OWN BODY

This argument is the one most frequently used by abortion advocates. The idea of the right to choose resonates with people's sense that everyone should be able to make their own choices in life. However, a person's right over his or her body is not absolute. For example, prostitution, illicit drugs, domestic abuse, and pornography are clear examples where a person's rights are not absolute. Although proponents of abortion state that the fetus is less than human, the woman's freedom should be severely limited if, in fact, the fetus is a person. Remember, the fetus is technically not a part of a woman's body. Although the fetus is developing inside a woman's body, it has its own genetic DNA and its own heart and circulatory system.

ARGUMENT #2: MAKING ABORTION ILLEGAL WOULD RETURN WOMEN TO THE BACK ALLEY ABORTION PROVIDERS

This argument has strong emotional appeal because no one wants to regress to a day and age where a woman's safety is placed in jeopardy. Of course, this argument assumes that the fetus is not a person. If the fetus is a person, a supporter of this argument would be making a case that society has the responsibility to make it safe to kill people who have the right to live in this world. This argument also overstates the danger of "back alley" abortions. Prior to 1973, 90 percent of illegal abortions were still performed by qualified doctors. The more shocking statistic is that since 1973, 1.5 million abortions are performed annually (prior to 1973 only 100,000 abortions were performed annually).

ARGUMENT #3: SOCIETY HAS NO RIGHT TO FORCE A WOMAN TO CARRY A PREGNANCY BEGUN BY RAPE OR INCEST

This is a very emotionally compelling argument. After all, a woman in this situation didn't simply forget to be careful with birth control. They were made pregnant without their consent—a truly horrific situation. As Christians we must be very careful when responding to this argument because we don't want to be uncaring toward the victim of such an awful plight. However, we must remember that the number of pregnancies that result from rape or incest is very small—roughly 1 in 100,000 cases. Finally, the violation of the woman could never justify the killing of another person in order to minimize the mental anguish of a violent trauma to a woman.

KEY ISSUE: WHEN DOES THE FETUS BECOME A PERSON?

Most philosophers believe that either the fetus is a person at the time of conception or that the fetus acquires this status at some point inside the woman. Here are the various suggestions for when a fetus possesses personhood.

First, many people, including the Supreme Court, use the concept of viability as the point when a fetus is granted the status of a person. Viability refers to the moment (24 to 26 weeks) when the fetus can live on its own. However, viability can never measure personhood precisely because technology constantly changes or varies from one culture to another. How can a fetus be a person in a more advanced culture and not a person in another, less medically advanced culture?

Second, others suggest that personhood is directly linked to a functioning brain (45 days). If cessation of brain activity (brain death) points to the death of a person, why not believe that the beginning of brain activity indicates personhood. Brain activity is limited as a measurement because an embryo has all the necessary potential for full brain activity, but it is just not yet realized.

Third, some believe that a fetus becomes a person at the moment they are capable of experiencing pain and other sensations. Experts call this sensation or feeling sentience. Sentience has some very problematic implications for a person in a vegetative state, comatose condition, or simply under anesthesia for surgery. Do people in those tragic conditions stop being a person?

Fourth, still others believe that the first time the mother feels the fetus inside of her (quickening) is a signal that the fetus has gained personhood.

Typically, Christians advocate that the fetus has full personhood from the moment of conception. The reasoning goes like this, courtesy of bio-ethics expert, Dr. Scott Rae:

- An adult human being is the end result of the continuous growth of the organism from conception.
- From conception to adulthood, this development has no break that is relevant to the essential nature of the fetus.
- Therefore, one is a human person from the point of conception onward.[132]

The following practical points can be helpful when trying to emphasize this idea. First, at the point of conception the fetus has its own genetic

---

132 Scott B. Rae, *Moral Choices: An Introduction to Ethics*, 142.

identity and has all the capabilities of becoming a functioning adult. Second, if a fetus is a person it becomes clear that the unborn child has a moral claim on the mother's body. In other words, the mother should provide whatever is necessary for the life of the child. Anyone would argue that a newborn child deserves the necessary resources to stay alive. If a mother refused to care for her newborn, she would be guilty of neglect or child abuse. In the same way, an unborn child has a claim on the mother. As Scott aptly comments, "If one concedes that the fetus is a person, then the only real difference between the fetus in the womb and the one-year-old is location."[133] Finally, our laws typically reflect a pro-life position. For example, the murder of a pregnant woman is a double homicide and a pregnant woman taking drugs is guilty of child abuse.

TIMELESS TRUTHS FOR A CULTURE THAT TEXTS

If a fetus has its own genetic identity and has all the capabilities to be a functioning adult, the unborn child has a moral claim on the mother's body.

---

[133] Scott B. Rae, 143.

Question 39
Is Physician Assisted Suicide Immoral?

In my 30 years as a pastor, I've witnessed the incredible grief and emotional burden that family members face as they watch loved one's experience immeasurable pain and suffering. Whether it is cancer, dementia, ALS or other debilitating diseases many families can only watch as their mother, father, or spouse waste away. I've seen people struggle with a sense of hopelessness where the only option is to witness the slow and agonizing decline of someone they love. As you watch people in the grips of a terminal illness, it's easy to understand why a growing number of people look to physician assisted suicide as a humane conclusion to the horrific struggle of unrelenting pain.

This is why the Pew Research Center indicated in their exhaustive report of November 2013 that a growing percentage of Americans believe individuals have a moral right to end their own lives.

> About six-in-ten adults (62%) say that a person suffering a great deal of pain with no hope of improvement has a moral right to commit suicide, up from 55% in 1990. A 56% majority also say this about those who have an incurable disease, up from 49% in 1990. While far fewer (38%) believe there is a moral right to suicide when someone is "ready to die because living has become a burden," the share saying this is up 11 percentage points, from 27% in 1990. About a third of adults (32%) say a person has a moral right to suicide when he or she "is an extremely heavy burden on his or her family," roughly the same share as in 1990 (29%).[134]

Despite the overwhelming struggle of watching those we love slide toward their physical death, we must be able to articulate the dividing line between what is moral and what is immoral. We have an obligation to protect the moral sensibilities of our nation—to prevent further harm to

---

134 Pew Research Center, November 2013 "Views on End-of-Life Medical Treatments", 7.

the moral fabric of America. The basic argument that physician-assisted suicide is immoral can be expressed in the following terms:

- Intentionally killing an innocent person always is morally wrong.
- Physician-assisted suicide is the intentional killing of an innocent person.
- Therefore, physician-assisted suicide is always morally wrong.

If a family member or friend asks why you believe physician-assisted suicide is immoral here are a handful of reasons that you might want to explain.

REASON #1: THERE IS A DIFFERENCE BETWEEN KILLING AND ALLOWING TO DIE

Advocates of physician-assisted suicide believe there is no significant difference between killing through physician-assisted suicide and allowing someone to die by the termination of life support. It's vital to recognize the place of "intent" in determining whether or not an action is moral or immoral. Everyone would recognize the difference between a gift and bribe—they are fundamentally different primarily because of the intent behind the identical acts. In the same way, intent clearly makes a moral difference between killing an innocent person and allowing a disease to take its natural course in a person's life. Listen to the viewpoint of esteemed former Supreme Court Chief Justice Rehnquist:

> When a patient refuses life sustaining medical treatment, he dies from an underlying fatal disease or pathology; but if a patient ingests lethal medication prescribed by a physician, he is killed by that medication.[135]

---

[135] Arthur J. Dyck, *Life's Worth: The Case Against Assisted Suicide* (Grand Rapids: Eerdmans, 2002), 37.

REASON #2: PAIN CAN BE TREATED WITHOUT PHYSICIAN-ASSISTED SUICIDE

Advocates of physician-assisted suicide insist that allowing patients to take their own life is the most merciful thing to do in order to stop needless suffering. The appeal to mercy or compassion for a loved one is one of the most common arguments for those who wish to embrace it. It's important to remember that with the advancement of pain-relief medication and the growing appeal of hospice care, many families have a greater assurance that the pain and suffering of their loved one can be treated effectively. Christian ethical expert Scott Rae describes it this way:

> The number of cases in which suffering prior to death is so severe that it cannot be adequately controlled is actually very small . . . . With available pain medication, virtually every patient's pain can be adequately managed. In the vast majority of cases, physician-assisted suicide or euthanasia is simply not necessary to fulfill the goal of medicine to provide relief of suffering.[136]

Please don't misunderstand what I am saying. I'm not trying to minimize unspeakable pain. I'm also not trying to argue that pain medications can always solve the problem of pain. Many families can tell horrific stories of the excruciating pain their loved one experienced during their battle with bone, pancreatic, or brain cancer. Sometimes there are no morally acceptable answers—we must walk with our family member through the shadow of death. My primary concern is that far too often people jump to the solution of physician-assisted suicide as the "only" solution without even considering whether this is morally acceptable.

REASON #3: PERSONAL AUTONOMY IS NOT ABSOLUTE

Advocates of physician-assisted suicide argue that there is a constitutional right to die. They believe that a person should have the ability to make their own decision about anything regarding their body. However, it's important to realize that there is no universal right to die.

---

[136] Scott B. Rae, Moral Choices: An Introduction to Ethics, 226.

The concept of absolute autonomy is not accurate—people are not allowed to do anything they wish.

- We don't let people kill themselves.
- We don't allow people to put illegal drugs into their body.
- We don't allow people to use their bodies for prostitution.
- We don't allow people to sell other human beings (human trafficking).
- We abolished practices of dueling to defend a person's honor/dignity.
- We don't allow someone to avenge a wrong by killing the perpetrator.

Finally, life itself runs counter to the idea of assisting people to kill themselves. When a child is brought into this world they are nurtured and protected—their life is valued. We expect that parents will be morally responsible in caring for their children. It is universally necessary to have laws, law enforcement agencies, and military forces in order to try to prevent killing and even threats to assault or kill human beings.

REASON #4: PEOPLE HAVE INTRINSIC VALUE

Some people don't believe in the intrinsic value of people. Rather, they believe that a person's identity is tied to a person's biographical life rather than a person's biological life. In other words, what really matters are "the sum of one's aspirations, decisions, activities, projects, and human relationships." Unfortunately, this view of personhood diminishes the intrinsic value of people. Are we to believe that the moment it becomes clear that a person's biographical life no longer has value then it is permissible to end a person's life voluntarily (via physician-assisted suicide) or involuntarily (euthanasia). Does this mean that certain patients (e.g., comatose patients or those in a persistent vegetative state) are of little intrinsic concern from a moral perspective? Does this mean that once a person no longer has the biographical life that it would be morally permissible to experiment on that person or brutalize them like the Nazis did to the Jews in WWII? If a person truly loses their identity when their biographical life is lost the slippery slope toward euthanasia has already begun.

REASON #5: PHYSICIAN-ASSISTED SUICIDE IS A SLIPPERY SLOPE

Physician-assisted suicide as a policy is a slippery slope. Should a person afflicted with a terminal illness may be allowed to take his or her life? Should this same person be permitted to authorize others to accomplish the same act simply because he is no longer able to perform the act?

Many of the decisions that revolve around end-of-life issues lack the kind of accountability that one would hope for in such an important ethical decision. There are already very disturbing studies being reported in Belgium and the Netherlands where physician-assisted suicide and euthanasia are legal. It's become clear that between 15% to 18% are done without the patient's knowledge. Opponents fear that candidates for euthanasia will include the non-terminally ill, such as people with Alzheimer's disease or other degenerative brain diseases, the severely mentally retarded, and the handicapped newborns.

TIMELESS TRUTHS FOR A CULTURE THAT TEXTS

There is a clear moral difference between killing an innocent person and allowing a disease to take its natural course in a person's life. Autonomy is not absolute--people are not allowed to do anything they wish.

Heaven and Hell

In our journey of faith, most Christians will eventually come face-to-face with the reality of the afterlife. A person may face a life-threatening disease, attempt to process the tragic loss of a loved one, or need to answer a friend with questions regarding the reality of a heaven or hell. Failure to prepare a Christian for these moments is a serious dereliction of our obligation to strengthen the faith of our brothers and sisters in Christ.

Because of our human frailty and fear of the unknown, the topic of death and the afterlife will always be difficult. Although we may struggle emotionally and physically with these issues, it's vital that we have some of the key answers so that our spiritual journey is not derailed or destroyed.

The concepts of heaven and hell invoke some of the most powerful reactions to people inside and outside the church. The concept of heaven as expressed in the following passage from Revelation brings universal hope and comfort of a better place in the presence of God:

> And I heard a loud voice from the throne saying, "Look! God's dwelling place is now among the people, and he will dwell with them. They will be his people, and God himself will be with them and be their God. 'He will wipe every tear from their eyes. There will be no

more death' or mourning or crying or pain, for the old order of things has passed away (Revelation 21:3-4)."

At the same time, the concept of hell can bring great dismay as well as outright confusion, especially as we read disturbing accounts in the Bible, such as, "They will be punished with everlasting destruction and shut out from the presence of the Lord and from the glory of his might (2 Thessalonians 1:9)."

Because this discussion is so difficult, we must give Christians the tools to better understand and explain these concepts. If not, people are in danger of not believing the Bible or simply coming to the conclusion that our faith is an expression of outdated morality and religion.

Question 40
Is There an Afterlife?

Recently, a friend of mine came up to me out of the blue and asked, "do you believe there is an afterlife?" I'm not sure what prompted his question. It may have been the failing health of his mother, the death of a sibling years earlier, or his own sense of mortality. Regardless of the motivation, I realized that he trusted me enough to ask me my opinion. I didn't quote a Bible verse. I didn't challenge his question. I didn't even judge him for having a legitimate doubt about the reality of the afterlife. I simply gave him an answer that would convey certain ideas yet be inviting enough that we could have another conversation in the future. It went something like this:

If there is no God—if we are simply the by-products of naturalistic evolution—then there probably isn't anything after this life because we die and that's it. However, I believe there is growing evidence from scientists and philosophers that God exists. If He exists, I believe it is reasonable to believe that there is something after this life. It seems to me that based upon that alone, it is very important to determine whether or not God really exists. In other words, there is a lot riding on it.

Far too often, our unchurched friends dismiss our religious conversation because they believe it is mere speculation, opinion, or preference. However, if we describe that we believe in the afterlife partly because of the growing evidence that God brought the universe into existence at a finite time in history, our discussion seems more reasonable. In addition, when we discuss the afterlife with friends, we must acknowledge that all of us face seasons in life where we consider the reality of death. It may be a personal illness, a current tragedy, or the trauma of a dying parent.

Each of these realities compels us to think about life and death. It's not always necessary to demand an immediate response, nor is it wise to put someone on the defensive by asking him whether he or she believes in the afterlife. My simple response to my friend ended our conversation in a way that sounded a lot like when you tell someone, "Catch you later." It reminded him that I am a safe person with whom to have a religious conversation. He was not ambushed. He was not compelled to make an immediate decision. Ultimately, it was an open invitation to keep talking. A year later when we talked about mutual friends facing cancer we had another conversation about heaven—it felt as natural as picking up a conversation with a life-long friend who came back into town.

As you think about talking to people about the afterlife here are some suggestions that may help you explain the reality of the afterlife.

EVIDENCE #1: MEANING OF LIFE

A Pew poll reported "that nearly 75 percent of Americans believe in heaven (defined as a place where people who have led good lives are eternally rewarded)."[137] Deep down inside, humanity is in a desperate search for the meaning of life. Viktor Frankl, who was a Nazi concentration camp survivor, believed that people were willing to sacrifice anything if there is a primary purpose for our sacrifice. Is it possible for a person to have an objective purpose in life without a final goal beyond death?

Many people live with a sense that their life has some deep and objective meaning to it. However, is it possible to have objective meaning if we are simply the by-product of naturalistic forces? If we are really not that different from the animals in the jungle, why would we possess belief in the afterlife? Maybe all of this points to the reality that we are not simply the by-product of purely naturalistic forces. Maybe it's time to realize that a sense of the eternal has been implanted into our souls by the hand of our immortal Creator (Romans 1:18-20).

For the person who doesn't believe in the afterlife, everything about their life and achievements will ultimately be buried under the debris of a dead universe and total annihilation. For a person who doesn't believe in either the soul or the afterlife, the universe and everything that exists is a cosmic accident. If God doesn't exist, life is utterly without any objective purpose or meaning.

---

[137] Jonathan Merritthttp://jonathanmerritt.religionnews.com/2016/01/01/heaven-and-near-death-experiences-separating-fact-from-fiction/

Tragically, modern man lives like there is genuine purpose to life, although they steadfastly deny it. The same is true of the afterlife and the soul. Francis Schaeffer explained this inconsistency with the following analogy:

> Modern man resides in a two-story universe. In the lower story is the finite world without God; here life is absurd, as we have seen. In the upper story are meaning, value, and purpose. Now modern man lives in the lower story because he believes there is no God. But cannot live happily in such an absurd world; therefore, he continually makes leaps of faith into the upper story to affirm meaning, value, and purpose, even though he has no right to, since he does not believe in God. Modern man is totally inconsistent when he makes this leap, because these values cannot exist without God, and man in his lower story does not have God.[138]

EVIDENCE #2: EXISTENCE OF THE SOUL

Many philosophers and scientists believe we are simply the by-product of physical processes. In other words, any thoughts, emotions, or pain are simply a reflection of the physical processes of a person's brain and nervous system. Of course, this has some huge implications. First, if I am just a physical brain, then the concept of existing outside my body is ridiculous. Any thought of the afterlife is nonsense. Second, if there is no soul, then any thought of free will is impossible. Everything we do is fixed by our environment, genetics, and chemistry. Philosopher Colin McGinn observes the following weakness in the argument that people are merely the by-products of naturalistic evolution:

> How can mere matter originate consciousness? How did evolution convert the water of biological tissue into the wine of consciousness? Consciousness seems like a radical novelty in the

---

[138] William Lane Craig, *Reasonable Faith: Christian Truth and Apologetics* (Chicago: Moody Press, 1984), 65.

> universe, not prefigured by the after-effects of the Big Bang; so how did it contrive to spring into being from what preceded it?[139]

The Bible teaches that every single person is made in the image of God and has both a body and a soul. Jesus affirmed the reality of the soul when He warned His disciples "not to fear those who can only kill the body; rather, we should fear Him who can destroy both body and soul (Matthew 10:28)."

The reality of the soul can be illustrated in several practical ways. First, imagine if a heroic Iraq war veteran returns from his service suffering from traumatic brain injuries and no longer has full function of the physical portion of his brain/mind. Do we consider him less than a full person? Of course not. Does this war veteran deserve full respect as an individual? Absolutely, because his identity is fundamentally immaterial. His identity is not solely based upon the function of certain parts of his physical body. Second, if a loved one is suffering from Alzheimer's, it is quite clear that they are limited in their cognitive ability to remember and to fully function in the physical realm. However, there is tremendous inherent value in this person because there is an immaterial part of every human being—the soul. Despite the degradation of the physical part of a person, they are still fully human.

Third, imagine the far reaching implications of many who experience near death experiences (NDE). What happens to the person who is temporarily brain dead? Many people describe their awareness of their surroundings during this period of time. One thing that might explain this sense of reality is that people have an immaterial part of their being which is called a soul.

In his bestselling book *Proof of Heaven: A Neurosurgeon's Journey into the Afterlife*, famous neurosurgeon Eben Alexander described how his own near death experience was not simply a fantasy produced by the

---

139 J.P. Moreland, *The Soul: How We Know It's Real and Why It Matters* (Chicago, Moody Publishers, 2014), 74.

brain under stress. It offered evidence that the soul uniquely possesses consciousness—it is not merely a function of one's brain chemistry.

EVIDENCE #3: THE NATURE OF GOD

The Christian faith teaches that God has eternally existed (Genesis 1:1; John 1:1). However, Christianity also teaches that God experienced eternal fellowship within His own essence as the Father, Son, and Holy Spirit (John 14:31; John 15:26; 1 John 5:11-12). The members of the Godhead decided that they would grant people the dignity of free will in hopes that they would choose to fellowship with God—both in this life and the next. Why would God who experiences eternal fellowship within the Trinity create humanity where our fellowship could only last during our short duration in this life? If God went to all this effort to send His own Son into the world (John 3:16), doesn't it make sense that He would desire to spend eternity with those who have embraced the sacrifice of Jesus and want to be with Him in Heaven?

EVIDENCE #4: CHRIST'S RESURRECTION

One of the most powerful statements by the greatest man who ever lived is found in the story of Lazarus when Jesus said, "I am the resurrection and the life. The one who believes in me will live, even though they die; **26** and whoever lives by believing in me will never die (John 11:25-26)." In that moment, Jesus revealed that He believed in the afterlife. However, He did much more than this. Jesus provided historical proof of the reality of those words at the moment that He rose from the dead. If Jesus can come back from physical death, then it is possible for Him to provide life for anyone after they die. If people have the capacity to live after physical death, then there is evidence for the immaterial part of man, the soul. Kreeft and Tacelli express the practical power of this argument with these words:

> Thus the Christian's answer to the most skeptical question of all, "what do you really know about life after death, anyway? Have you

ever been there? Have you come back to tell us?" is "No, but I have a very good Friend who has."[140]

TIMELESS TRUTHS FOR A CULTURE THAT TEXTS

If God created the world with the purpose of fellowship with people, wouldn't He have created the afterlife to continue this fellowship?

[140] Peter Kreeft and Ronald K. Tacelli, *Handbook of Christian Apologetics*, 255.

Question 41
Why Didn't God Simply Place People in Heaven?

Many people look at the rampant evil throughout our world and ask, "If God created a perfect place like heaven, why didn't He simply place all of us in heaven?" It's important to remember that this isn't a wrong question because God actually chose to create angels and place them in heaven. Here are several different approaches that might prove helpful.

First, God has granted people the dignity of free will. Our free choice not only dictates everything about our life here on earth, it also determines our existence in the afterlife. Simply put, the experience of our world and our entrance into heaven are both based upon the dignity of free will. God is simply not able to bypass the dignity of free will and place us in heaven without our choice. God even respected the free will of those angelic beings (1/3 of the heavenly host) who decided to join Lucifer in rejecting Him (Isaiah 14:12-14; Hebrews 12:22).

Second, everyone has a choice on whether or not they can live in the presence of God. Scripture is clear that people can choose to live with God (John 1:12; 3:16). In creating the world, God chose not to interfere with mankind's free choice. Ultimately, God will make the same decision for eternity. Heaven is not a place in which a person with free will can be placed—it must be chosen. Influential Christian philosopher and thinker, William Lane Craig makes this observation:

> It's logically impossible to make someone freely do something. God's being all-powerful doesn't mean that He can do the logically impossible. Thus, even though He is all-powerful, God cannot make everyone freely be saved. Given human freedom and human stubbornness, some people may go to hell despite God's desire and efforts to save them.[141]

---

[141] William Lane Craig and Ray Bradley, "The Craig-Bradley Debate," accessed March 25, 2015.

Third, people must not only choose to be with God we must also choose to be like God. Romans 8 tells us that one of God's over-arching purposes for this life is to conform everyone to the image of Jesus Christ. Much of life is not good in and of itself. It is full of terrible and horrific things, but we are told that God is able to use an imperfect world for a greater good—to conform as many people as possible into the image of His Son.

> 28 And we know that in all things God works for the good of those who love him, who have been called according to his purpose. 29 For those God foreknew he also predestined to be conformed to the likeness of his Son, that He might be the first-born among many brethren;
> Romans 8:28-29

For God to produce people who are in the process of being like Him in every facet of their lives—an idealistic playpen is simply not the kind of world that achieves these goals. If your children or grandchildren never faced any difficulty or adversity they would become ethically and morally disfigured. We see this principle lived out every single day. Sometimes it is necessary to allow suffering in a person's life in order to bring about some greater good. Doctors often must inflict painful procedures and treatments on people for the purpose of better health and longer life. Parents take away toys and privileges which cause pain because they want their child to grow up with self-control. In many cases, the difficult situations can actually cultivate our character or open up opportunities we never thought possible.

For years, Soviet cosmonauts struggled in the aftermath of space voyages. It was not uncommon for the cosmonauts to spend 200 to 300 days in space. Upon their return to earth they suffered from dizziness, high pulse rates, and heart palpitations. They couldn't walk for a week, and after 30 days, they were still undergoing therapy for weakened muscles and hearts. The problem was simple. At zero gravity, the muscles of the body begin to waste away because there is no resistance. It became necessary for scientists to design the penguin suits which was a running suit laced with elastic bands. It resisted every move the cosmonauts made, forcing them to exert their strength. God has allowed this very imperfect world to operate as our very own penguin suit. However undesired--hurtful times are used by God to develop that part of our lives which struggles through the imperfectness of life itself. This imperfect world gives us the choice to be with God and to be like God.

Third, when God created Adam and Eve they were placed within a pristine and innocent environment called the Garden of Eden. Unfortunately, they chose to rebel against God's moral will for the universe. Although the Garden of Eden was not a perfect place like heaven, it was clearly an untarnished place. This was an idealistic location (heaven on earth) yet the first humans rejected it because they chose their own path rather than God's path. Every single human being has done the same thing—they have chosen the same path of independence, rebellion, and sinfulness as the original couple.

God has chosen our world as a place where people can enjoy the dignity of free will in this life. However, our free will is not only a reality in this life—it also functions in heaven. William Lane Craig describes the connection this way:

> God's purpose is not restricted to this life but spills over beyond the grave into eternal life. According to Christianity, this life is but the cramped and narrow foyer opening up into the great hall of God's eternity. God promises eternal life to all those who place their trust in in Christ as Savior and Lord.[142]

TIMELESS TRUTHS FOR A CULTURE THAT TEXTS

Heaven is not a place in which a person with free will can be placed—it must be chosen.

[142] William Lane Craig, *Hard Questions, Real Answers* (Wheaton: Crossway, 2003), 97.

Question 42
Is Eternal Punishment Fair?

For most of my Christian journey, I didn't think through all the implications of hell. It was simply the logical opposite of the place called heaven. If heaven was the place where people can enjoy the presence of a perfect Creator, then hell must be a place totally devoid of the goodness, morality, and kindness of God. However, for the last ten years the question on whether hell is fair has continually dogged my steps. It's not that I've questioned the teaching of Scripture. It's not that I have doubted the realities of the afterlife. It's just that I can't run away from the inherent difficulty of the topic of hell. I can't ignore it. I feel the personal implications of people I know and love. At times, it feels like the ache in my heart will not go away. C.S. Lewis echoed some of my emotions on hell:

> This doctrine is one of the chief grounds on which Christianity is attacked as barbarous and the goodness of God impugned. We are told that it is a detestable doctrine—and indeed, I too detest it from the bottom of my heart. . . . I am not going to try to prove the doctrine tolerable. Let us make no mistake; it is not tolerable. But I think the doctrine can be shown to be moral.[143]

Theologian John Feinberg expressed the difficulty that Christians face as we try to explain hell:

> Prior to the twentieth century, humans had seen various forms of inhumanity perpetrated against other persons. . . . But then came the absolute brutality of World War I, and if that wasn't enough, World War II was even more horrible. And, it was accompanied by the Holocaust. Many have asked how there could possibly be an all-loving and omnipotent God who would allow such evils. For many, the horrors of the Holocaust were the final nails in the coffin of anything like traditional theism. Despite the enormity of such evil, for many the existence of hell is an even worse blow to the credibility of

---

[143] C.S. Lewis, *The Problem of Pain* (Waukegan, IL; Fontana Press, 1967), 107.

> theism. . . . If you think it is hard to justify a holocaust in this life, just try to justify a never ending holocaust in the next life![144]

Unfortunately, many philosophers and theologians attempt to resolve this issue by suggesting that everyone will either be saved or that people will be annihilated so that they won't have to face eternal punishment. Here are some brief thoughts about each of these viewpoints.

EVERYONE WILL BE SAVED

There are a handful of reasons why Christians should be cautious in thinking that Scripture teaches that everyone will be saved. First, if people have free choice, there can't be any guarantees about whether or not they will eventually respond to God's love. Scripture clearly teaches that even Jesus Christ was not able to convince some in the nation of Israel to follow Him (Matthew 23:37). It would seem odd that the Scripture would provide an example of something that Jesus can't do when God will eventually prove that He can do it. Second, it's not necessary for all the souls in our world to turn to God for this to be a morally good world. Down through the centuries, millions of people have responded to God's love and have become the kind of people that He always intended us to become. Third, God is not obligated to do everything possible to win a person back to Him. He is only obligated to act with love toward His creatures. The simple truth is that God can never ensure that a person will respond with actions that are good and not evil.

THOSE WHO REJECT GOD WILL BE ANNIHILATED

Some Christians believe that those who reject God to the very end of life will ultimately be destroyed by God (annihilated). Those who have claimed Jesus as their Savior will live forever because they have placed their trust in Christ for their eternal destiny. Those who reject Christ are not consigned to eternal punishment. God simply destroys them, which

---

144 John S. Feinberg, *The Many Faces of Evil: Theological Systems and the Problems of Evil*, 395.

prevents them from experiencing eternal life with Him in heaven. Many thinkers believe this is a more just punishment for rejecting God in one's lifetime. Although annihilation tries to remove the difficulty of hell, it is not consistent with the teaching of the Bible. Scripture teaches that the fates of both the saved and unsaved last forever. This is the clear implication of Jesus when He taught, "And these will go away into eternal punishment, but the righteous into eternal life (Matthew 25:46)." In addition, the Bible reveals that one's eternal destiny is predicated on the choice of an individual. Man's free will—even in regard to one's eternal destiny—cannot be violated by God.

In the absence of explaining away the reality of hell, it's important that the Christian have a reasonable explanation for why an all-loving and all-powerful God can embrace the concept of hell.

First, heaven offers eternal joy and fellowship with God (Revelation 22:3-5). Hell as its opposite offers eternal separation and lack of joy. A place totally devoid and absent of the presence of God must be a place of great anguish and frustration.

Second, the Bible teaches that no one will be sentenced to hell as a result of a lack of evidence. In the parable of Lazarus, the rich man pleads for someone to rise from the dead to warn his family. However, Abraham reminds him that someone who is not willing to listen to the evidence around them (Old Testament prophets) will not even listen to someone who comes back from the dead. Jesus used this story to paint a very clear picture—the testimony of the Old Testament (v.16) was sufficient evidence for a person who was pursuing the truth about Christ. This was also quite clear from the behavior and response of the Pharisees as they explained away the message of Jesus while continually asking for more signs (Luke 11:16). Although Jesus raised someone from the dead who bore witness to His identity the Pharisees tried to kill both Jesus and Lazarus (John 11:45-53, 12:10-11).

Third, people who break the moral law of an infinitely perfect God must find a way to atone for their offense. The biggest question is how does a person account for breaking the moral law of an infinitely perfect God? The world religions say you simply do good, but think of how absurd this would be in a court of law. Imagine attempting to avoid any penalties for running a red light and causing a horrible accident by promising to only go through green lights in the future. This would never pay the debt incurred the one time you were caught breaking the law by going through a red light, would it? Having broken the law, God justly judges us. When we offend God who is an infinite, holy being, the debt that is incurred becomes eternal. How do you pay an eternal infinite debt? A substitute is needed since we cannot pay an infinite debt. Only an infinite person who is both God and man can pay an infinite debt. This is exactly what Jesus Christ has provided for all of humanity.

Fourth, Christianity is routinely criticized for its belief in such a horrible place like hell. People don't believe it's fair. However, compared to many other religions, the God of the Bible is not asking a lot. Christianity is the only religion that allows the worst into God's heaven by virtue of His own grace. He says that He has such a great desire for all of humanity to join Him in a perfect place that He sent His own Son to die on the cross in our place. In addition, He says that a sinner can ask for forgiveness based upon the death of Christ. We don't have to earn our way to heaven or achieve a certain religious code. Every sinner is welcome. Obviously, hell is very sad but not unfair. In a society that is constantly asking for free stuff or a hand up—Christianity offers the ultimate free gift.

Fifth, the Bible teaches that hell is a place where people will continue to demonstrate their resistance, disobedience, and hatred for God (Revelation 16:9). Sins committed in this life and in eternity merit infinite punishment. Of course, no one commits an infinite number of sins in his or her earthly life. However, sin in this life or the afterlife cannot go unpunished since God is perfectly just. Punishment must continue because sinning continues to happen throughout eternity as people reject God and His standard.

Sixth, separation from society is reserved for the most serious crimes. The most serious crime—murder—is punishable by the most severe sanction, which is being separated from society for life in prison. To defy and disregard God and to disobey His law for the duration of one's life should result in separation from God and his people. For a person who has ignored God throughout their entire life, it might not only be fair but also just for that person to be eternally separated from God. It's important to remember that sin is the process by which people become enslaved to anything that takes the place of God Himself. Keller puts it this way:

> Modern people struggle with the idea of God's thinking up punishments to inflict on disobedient people. When sin is seen as slavery and hell as the freely chosen, eternal skid row of the universe, hell becomes much more comprehensible.[145]

A person can be so enslaved to things (work, achievement, and autonomy) that they never wish to give them up—even if it means that they eternally refuse the overtures of God.

Finally, we must remember that our goal is not just to communicate the awful reality of hell. We have the opportunity to illustrate the concept of Christ's love by illustrating the pain and anguish that Jesus experienced on the cross, which was His own version of hell. Hell is a way to communicate the magnitude of Christ's love for humanity. Pastor Timothy Keller is one of the most empathetic yet intelligent pastors in America. He has provided invaluable insight on how to help different segments of the church better connect to and understand God's rationale behind hell. He describes how he has personally communicated the concept of hell:

> Unless we come to grips with this terrible doctrine, we will never even begin to understand the depths of what Jesus did for us on the cross. His body was being destroyed in the worst possible way, but that was a flea bite compared to what was happening to his soul. When he cried out that his God had forsaken him, he was experiencing hell itself. If a mild acquaintance denounces you and rejects you—that hurts. If a good friend does the same—the hurt's far worse. However, if your spouse walks out on you, saying, "I never want to see you again," that is far more devastating still. The longer, deeper, and more intimate the relationship, the more

---

[145] Timothy Keller, "Preaching Hell in a Tolerant Age", Leadership Journal, http://www.christianitytoday.com/le/1997/fall/7l4042.html.

torturous is any separation. But the Son's relationship with the Father was beginning-less and infinitely greater than the most intimate and passionate human relationship. When Jesus was cut off from God, he went into the deepest pit and most powerful furnace, beyond all imagining. And he did it voluntarily, for us.[146]

TIMELESS TRUTHS FOR A CULTURE THAT TEXTS

In a world where God grants people the dignity of free will, He must grant people their wish to have nothing to do with His will or His presence.

[146] Timothy Keller, "Preaching Hell in a Tolerant Age", Leadership Journal, http://www.christianitytoday.com/le/1997/fall/7l4042.html.

World Religions

There is a heated debate about the overall impact of religion upon society. Some believe it is a force for good while others claim it is a misguided force for evil and hate. Noted atheist Richard Dawkins writes: "Faith can be very, very dangerous, and deliberately to implant it into the vulnerable mind of an innocent child is a grievous wrong."[147] In contrast, James Gaston, a professor of history and humanities at the Franciscan University of Steubenville says:

> My argument is simply stated: religion is not only good for society, but it is essential to society. . . . Religion is good and thus essential to society because of you...Everyone must search for truth, for self-knowledge...for God. We differ in what we think such happiness exists. Nonetheless, we search.[148]

---

[147] Richard Dawkins, *The God Delusion*, https://www.washingtonpost.com/posteverything/wp/2015/01/14/is-religion-a-force-for-good.

[148] James Gaston in Maggie Maslak, "Is Religion Good or Bad Society? Two Experts Debate, http://www.catholicnewsagency.com/news/is-religion-good-or-bad-for-society-two-experts-debate-56023/

Religion has had a powerful impact upon the history of humanity—both bad and good. The abuse and distortion of religious beliefs has led to the slaughter and genocide of millions of people. The embrace of religious values has also brought comfort and compassion to hurting people in every country and at every period of human history. We live in a religiously diverse world. We are surrounded by people of various cultures, viewpoints, and religions.

As Christians, we are obligated by God's Word "to contend for the faith that was once for all entrusted to God's holy people (Jude 3)." In a gracious and non-judgmental fashion, God has asked us to clarify the distinctions and correct the errors of the world religions, and make sure that people are provided clear and reasonable evidences for the truth of the good news of Jesus Christ. As an expert of worldwide religions, James A. Beverley reminds us of the necessity of comparing Christianity with the religions of the world:

> Christians must recognize the contradictions and ultimate disunity that exist among the religions of the world. Contrary to popular opinions, the religions of the world often disagree—even on basic points. For example, Buddhists do not believe in God. Jews and Muslims do not accept the Trinity. Mormon males believe they will progress to Godhood in eternity. Unificationists believe that Sun Myung Moon is the Messiah. Jehovah's Witnesses trust the Watchtower Society alone for spiritual guidance. . . . What should be obvious in the study of religions is their lack of similarity rather than their alleged unity.[149]

[149] James A. Beverley, *Nelson's Illustrated Guide to Religions* (Nashville: Thomas Nelson, 2009), 9.

Question 43
Is Mormonism Christian?

Every four years during the Presidential election season we watch as candidates, parties, and political action groups spend millions of dollars to make sure that their candidate is painted in the best possible light while the candidate from the opposite party is defined in the worst possible light. Of course, this is tremendously important if a candidate is trying to change long-held perceptions of what they are like or what political positions they have held.

The same thing happens within the realm of religion. Many times it is necessary for religious groups to rebrand themselves in order to remove some of the negative perceptions that people have of their teaching or tactics. No religion has been more successful in this effort than the Church of Jesus Christ of Latter-day Saints.

The movement to legitimize Mormonism was highlighted on a national stage when Mitt Romney, a practicing Mormon, ran for President of the United States in 2012. His Mormon faith was presented as part of the religious mainstream of America. In fact, Mormonism has made a huge publicity push by scholars, pundits, and politicians to convince people that they are Christians and not a group that teaches heretical doctrines.

Mormons claim to believe in Christ, they claim He is their savior, and they claim to be the best representation of the church of Jesus Christ. In light of these claims and due to the fact that for decades the Christian church has viewed Mormonism as a cult, it's vital that Christians have the ability to challenge the claim that Mormonism is Christian.

Whenever a religion claims to be distinctly Christian, we have to evaluate their beliefs based upon the 2,000-year-old historic claims of Christianity. The easiest way to challenge these claims is to ask two basic questions of Mormonism in order to see whether or not their views match the orthodox claims of the Christianity.

CHRISTIAN VIEW OF GOD

Orthodox Christianity claims that God is an eternal being. God did not come into existence but has always existed as God. He is a self-existent being who has no prior cause or end. In addition, He is outside the normal time constraints of a finite being. As the unique Supreme Being of the universe, God knows all things and sustains the universe (Psalm 90:2; 1 Timothy 1:17; John 1:18). Orthodox Christianity also claims that God is essentially a spirit and not a physical being.

The Mormon view of God is clearly different than the historic and orthodox Christian viewpoint. Mormonism claims that God the Father was once a mortal man who continually progressed to become a god. Mormonism teaches that humans are literally the younger siblings of Jesus since every human existed in another world before they were born on Earth.

At first glance, it might appear that Mormonism has more in common with paganism than the historic Christian doctrine of God. Listen to this description of the Mormon doctrine of God, which has the ring of pagan truths:

- Plurality of Gods: not just the God of the Bible
- God is not eternal; He came into existence
- God is an exalted man
- God is not the creator of the universe; simply the God of our world

Mormonism is not in keeping with orthodox views related to the nature of God. Although Mormons love to use the same Christian verbiage, their views about God appear to blend polytheism and New Age beliefs. Beverley makes this observation:

> The Mormon view that there is more than one God is contradicted by clear biblical teaching in Deuteronomy 4:35, Isaiah 44:6-8, and John 17:3, among hundreds of other verses in the Bible that teach that only one God exists. . . . Further, the Mormon notion that God used to be a man is a stunning aberration from the mind of Joseph Smith. . . . That God is not a man is taught in Malachi 3:6 and Isaiah 44:6. Likewise, the Mormon view that God has a body of flesh and

bones is contrary to Psalm 139:7-10, Jeremiah 23:24, and John 4:24.[150]

CHRISTIAN VIEW OF SALVATION

Christianity claims that the entirety of our salvation is by grace through faith, not by works (Ephesians 2:8-9; Galatians 2:16). Christianity claims that at the moment we place our trust in Christ's finished work on the cross that we are declared righteous before God. All humanity has sinned (Romans 3:23) by virtue of their fallen nature and their flawed actions. Mankind's sin has created a spiritually bankrupt relationship between humanity and a perfect God (Romans 6:23). The tremendous message of the gospel is that the death and resurrection of Jesus affords human beings the opportunity to be forgiven for their sins.

Mormon teaching differs from the Biblical teaching of salvation. Mormonism claims that individual salvation results from obedience to the laws of the gospel. God's grace alone does not save. While Christians view salvation as a gift, Mormons view it as a loan. In other words, Jesus pays for our sins up front (and thus they call him "Savior"), but we have to pay him back for what he did with our good works.

The Mormon version of salvation is taught using an analogy involving a benefactor who relieves a debtor from a huge debt. In exchange for keeping him from prison and paying his debts, the debtor must now keep the terms of the contract. In the Mormon worldview this analogy means that the person must repent and keep God's commandments if he or she is going to live with Him.

When Christians talk about salvation they mean that mankind is permanently and fully saved from the effects of sin. The word salvation refers to God's solution to the morally flawed condition of mankind. It describes how people can be declared righteous in the sight of God. When Christians talk about atonement they are referring to the sacrifice of Jesus the God/Man on the cross. It was a sacrifice that placed all the

---

[150] James A. Beverley, *Nelson's Illustrated Guide to Religions,* 375.

sins of mankind upon the perfect Christ. It bridged the moral gap between flawed people and a perfect God.

When Mormons talk about salvation they essentially mean resurrection. Mormons call Jesus "Savior" because He saved the human race from physical death. People are saved because they are given the chance to achieve the goal of becoming a "god." When Mormons talk about the atonement of Jesus they refer to the act of Jesus overcoming physical death for the human race. They are talking about removing the sin barrier between man and God.

Stephen Covey, a devout Mormon and best-seller author of *The Seven Habits of Highly Effective People* describes the Mormon viewpoint with these disturbing words:

> I have found in speaking to various non-LDS groups in different cultures that we can teach and testify of many gospel principles (i.e. Mormonism) if we are careful in selecting words which carry our meaning but from their experience and frame of mind. . . . Salvation by grace alone—the mainstay of salvation—is a false concept and an apostate doctrine.[151]

These strong words clearly illustrate the difference between historic Christianity and the views of the Church of Jesus Christ of Latter-day Saints.

TIMELESS TRUTHS FOR A CULTURE THAT TEXTS

A movement can't claim to be uniquely Christian if their view of God and salvation is drastically different from historic Christianity.

---

[151] Stephen R. Covey, *The Divine Center: Why We Need a Life Centered on God and Christ and How We Attain It* (Salt Lake City: Deseret Books, 2004), 240.

Question 44
Is the Teaching of Jehovah's Witnesses Biblical?

Imagine the scene in the fourth century. Three centuries of bitter and vicious persecution of the Christian faith had finally come to a halt. The greatest leaders of the church from around the world—many of them still bearing the scars of persecution—were gathered. The most prominent person in the whole world, Constantine, who was the Emperor of the Roman Empire, was the featured guest. This incredible scene described the greatest challenge to our understanding of the person of Jesus Christ. It was called the Council of Nicaea, and it took place in AD 325. The purpose of calling this council was to denounce the heretical views of a man by the name of Arius and a movement that came to be known as Arianism.

Arius preached that the Second Person of the Trinity, who is known to us as Jesus Christ, was not truly equal to the Father, nor could he be "true God of true God." He was, according to Arius, nothing more than a creature immensely more perfect than any other creature, but a creature nonetheless. As a result of this Council, the church condemned Arias and his teachings. The church thought this heresy had been effectively removed. However, in the late 1800s, a form of Arianism attempted once more to spread itself within the confines of the church. This movement was called Jehovah's Witnesses.

Although there are countless verses which demonstrate the doctrinal deficiencies of Jehovah's Witnesses, this chapter will focus on one single verse. The first verse of the Gospel of John is essential if a Christian desires to master a Biblical understanding of Christ. John 1:1 says, "In the beginning was the Word, and the Word was with God, and the Word was God." It contains the following truths that eloquently describe the divine nature of Jesus Christ.

- Christ has existed throughout eternity: "In the beginning was the Word." The expression "Word" is literally the Greek word *logos*. *Logos* was used technically within Greek philosophy to describe the all-pervasive mind which ruled and gave meaning to all things. This simple phrase tells us that before time began, the Word—the self-existent one—had always existed.

- Christ has a distinct personality: "and the Word was with God." The Apostle John was given the responsibility of faithfully describing the complex nature of God. To accurately explain Jesus, he had to provide us with a brief glimpse of the Trinity—the complex nature of God. By using the tiny little Greek word "with" John was trying to stress that the Word was a distinct individual in the presence of God.

- Christ has the very nature of God: "and the Word was God." The third line of John's description adds a needed exclamation point to his discussion. Just in case there were any doubts, John wanted to stress that Christ has the very nature of God.

In the face of their insistence that Jesus was only the first of God's created beings and fundamentally inferior to Almighty God, Jehovah's Witnesses have attempted to rewrite John 1:1 based upon their own translation of the New Testament called the New World Translation. They claim that because there is no definite article in the Greek language in the last line that the last phrase of this verse should be changed from "God" to "a god." In other words, they believe the verse stops talking about Almighty God of the universe and begins discussing an inferior god.

Allow me to explain briefly how a person should respond to this clever distortion of the Bible. The Greek definite article, the English word "the," is predominately used as a pointer. For example, take a quick look at these two statements and see if you can tell the difference:

- "I need the Bible": If I say I need the Bible, I'm stressing that I would like a particular or specific Bible that I'm thinking about. Often you use the word "the" as if you are pointing at a particular Bible that you are looking at.
- "I need a Bible": The focus is on any book that has the quality of being a Bible; it's not pointing to a particular one. Rather, it's simply asking that you give me a book that has as its very essence or quality—the nature of being God's Word.

This is exactly what the Apostle John was doing in John 1:1. John did not accidently omit the definite article in the last phrase of verse 1. In his wisdom, he was laying a foundation for a correct understanding of the complex nature of God (Trinity). Here's what the Apostle John was trying to communicate:

- When the article is used (2nd line of verse 1), the emphasis of the word is on individuality. John is pointing to the Word as a person—the individuality of the Word standing next to God the Father.
- Without the article (3rd line of verse 1) the emphasis of the word is on quality. John is pointing to the very essence of the Word—the Word contains the very nature of God.

Jehovah's Witnesses are pretty unaware of this distinction. For example, if you examined all the places in the first eighteen verses of John's Gospel where the Greek article is absent before the term "God" you would expect to find that the Jehovah's Witnesses translate these "a god." However, they don't. They are totally inconsistent. The following references in the same chapter of the same Gospel of John contain the term "God" without the article:

- There came a man who was sent from God; his name was John (John 1:6).
- Yet to all who received him, to those who believed in his name, he gave the right to become children of God (John 1:12).
- Children born not of natural descent, nor of human decision or a husband's will, but born of God (John 1:13).
- No one has ever seen God, but God the One and Only, who is at the Father's side, has made him known (John 1:18).

If you're talking to your Jehovah's Witness friend, you need to get your Bible out and turn to these four verses. Ask them a simple question. If you insist on making the Word mean a lesser type of god in verse 1 simply on the basis that it doesn't have the Greek article, why aren't you consistent with all these other verses?

TIMELESS TRUTHS FOR A CULTURE THAT TEXTS

The Bible is crystal clear that Christ was more than a mere man or the most perfect creature created by God. He existed throughout eternity and possesses every quality that defines God.

Question 45
Is Scientology a Cult?

Webster's Dictionary defines a cult as "a small religious group that is not part of a larger and more accepted religion and that has belief regarded by many people as extreme or dangerous."[152] Christianity enhances this definition by describing a cult in the following fashion:

> In a Christian context, the definition of a cult is, specifically, "a religious group that denies one or more of the fundamentals of biblical truth." A cult is a group that teaches doctrines that, if believed, will cause a person to remain unsaved. A cult claims to be part of a religion, yet it denies essential truth(s) of that religion. Therefore, a Christian cult will deny one or more of the fundamental truths of Christianity while still claiming to be Christian.[153]

Although it is not wise to offend people of other religious faiths, it's accurate to describe the Church of Scientology as a religious cult. Although it's not necessary to use this term when talking to a member of Scientology because of its inflammatory nature, there are a handful of reasons why a Christian is justified in making this assessment.

First, Scientology clearly involves cult-like behavior such as spying and video-taping, black-mailing, exclusion from family, and penalties for leaving the church. The BBC produced *The Secrets of Scientology* in 2010, which provided clear evidence of cult-like behavior.[154]

Second, believers of Scientology have a well-documented allegiance to its founder L. Ron Hubbard and to their current leader, David Miscavige. This allegiance is fanatical and no member of Scientology is allowed to question its teaching. L. Ron Hubbard became popular when he published his famous book, *Dianetics*. Under its present leader, Scientology has enjoyed tremendous success, growth, and popularity.

---

152 "Simple Definition of Cult" http://www.merriam-webster.com/dictionary/cult.

153 http://www.gotquestions.org/cult-definition.html.

154 https://www.youtube.com/watch?v=L0vtBFGcU4c.

One of the powerful drawing points for this religious group is the following of mega-Hollywood stars such as John Travolta and Tom Cruise.

Third, Scientology presents a radically different worldview of reality than historic Christianity. In fact, this religious group makes little or no attempt to integrate Jesus into any of their material or paradigms. Scientology bases their philosophy/teaching upon the teaching of L. Ron Hubbard—not Jesus Christ. Scientology looks at humanity and salvation in a dramatically different fashion than Christianity. Here is a brief summary of their core teaching:

- Human beings are immortal (Scientology uses the term thetans).
- Human beings must reach their potential or true identity as thetans (many causes prevent them from seeing their true identity).
- Human beings are assisted in the ultimate goal of being an Operating Thetan (OT) by going through "auditing" counseling. In these sessions, a person is assisted in keeping track of the workings of their inner identity by use of an e-meter.

Scientology's stated goal of helping a person reach his or her true human potential is very attractive in a self-help culture but absolutely contrary to the core teachings of Christianity. Their view that every single human being has always existed is diametrically opposed to the teachings of Christianity. In addition, their concept of salvation is not in any way rooted in the sacrifice of Christ on the cross or viewed through the lens of man's need to atone for their sin before a moral God.

TIMELESS TRUTHS FOR A CULTURE THAT TEXTS

Scientology is a cult and denies the classic truth of Christianity—salvation through the cross of Christ.

Question 46
How Should Christians Respond to Islam?

The United States of America just paused to remember the 15th anniversary of the World Trade Centers' terrorist attacks on September 11, 2001. Nearly 3,000 people in New York, Virginia, and Pennsylvania lost their lives in attacks carried out using hijacked airplanes overtaken by terrorists and orchestrated by Osama bin Laden. Unfortunately, those events continue to haunt and frighten people. We live in a world inflamed by the horrific actions of ISIS, and with the many other terrorist groups that fall under the label of radical Islamic extremism. People are frightened that terrorism might launch another large scale attack or lone-wolf attacks. We live in troubling times where death and terror can happen unexpectedly anywhere on the globe.

At the same time, Christians have been called to have a balanced and gracious response to the Islamic community. There are millions of Muslims who live in America and embrace our culture, live in peace, and deplore the efforts of extreme groups that attempt to impose their version of Islam upon the world. As the Islamic population in America continues to grow, we have a deep responsibility to be salt and light to our Islamic friends, neighbors, and co-workers.

There are many factors that have made it hard for Christians to maintain a God-honoring balance between being alert and cautious versus being salt and light. Some Christians have difficulty identifying the core differences between Christianity and Islam. Other Christians struggle in resolving the abusive history of Muhammad and the global ambition of Islam. Most Christians don't know how to evangelize Muslims when there is so much confusion and violence that surrounds the Muslim ideology. This chapter will focus briefly on each of these issues.

First, Islam is diametrically different and opposed to Christianity in the one area that can't be ignored—Jesus. Christianity claims that Jesus died for the sins of humanity. Islam denies that Jesus is the Son of God and that He died on the cross. This simple difference illustrates why Islam and Christianity can't both be right; one of them is clearly wrong. Either the crucifixion of Jesus of Nazareth happened or it didn't happen. Muslims are faced with a very daunting task. Their claim that Jesus wasn't crucified flies in the face of secular and religious evidence that convincingly demonstrates the crucifixion of Jesus as a historical fact. They expect the modern world to deny the historic reality of the crucifixion based upon a few verses written by the Prophet Muhammad six hundred years after the death of Jesus.

Second, the exclusive truth claims of the Christian faith are based upon the simple fact that Christianity is the only religion fundamentally established on the basis of God's grace and not any meritorious religious works. The Islamic understanding of salvation is diametrically opposed to the Christian doctrine of salvation by faith alone and grace alone (Ephesians 2:8-9). It's important to note that the average Muslim carries the everyday burden of wondering if their adherence to the Qur'an and the example of Muhammad is sufficient for salvation. In addition, the Islamic view of the sovereign will of Allah in regard to salvation is another powerful reminder that the average Muslim cannot be certain of their eternal destiny.

Third, although Christians should have no interest in disparaging religious leaders of other faiths, there have always been serious concerns and reservations about the prophet Muhammad. It's not simply the glaring lack of accurate information concerning the crucifixion of Christ and the reliability of the New Testament Scriptures. In contrast to the peace and kindness of Jesus the Messiah, Muhammad's life shows a very different picture that all too often disturbs the modern world. This is especially true as people see some of these same qualities exhibited by people across the globe. The imminent evangelical expert on religion, James Beverley reminds us of several disturbing aspects of the prophet's life:

> The Christian tradition has always had enormous difficulty with the following aspects of Muhammad's life: (a) episodes of extreme brutality both in war and in dealing with some of his enemies, (b) his lack of tolerance toward critics and those who chose not to follow

> Islam, (c) his adoption of polygamy and arrogance toward his wives, especially by use of his prophetic status to crush dissent.[155]

Fourth, there are facts about the nature of Islam that create tremendous anxiety for both Christian and unbeliever alike. James A. Beverley cites the following facts:

- The Qur'an uses the term jihad in terms of spiritual struggle.
- The Qur'an also uses the term jihad to mean holy war or just war.
- The Prophet engaged in battles of war.
- The Prophet taught that Islam must be spread to the whole world.
- Islamic law justifies self-defense and certain acts of war.
- Muslims divide the world into two: Islam and non-Islam.
- Many Muslims believe that all countries should follow Islamic law.
- Many Muslim countries are non-democratic and crush dissent.[156]

On the surface, these facts/realities are more than a little alarming. It's easy to recognize why both Christians and non-Christians might look at these facts and become terribly concerned regarding the growing influence of Islam throughout the world. It's important to note that these facts have been interpreted by the worldwide Muslim community in two different ways. The vast majority of Muslims believe that none of these facts justify the horrific actions of Islamic terrorism in the world. However, radical Muslim extremists point to these same facts and believe they not only justify their actions but lay a foundation for terrorism throughout the world.

The collective weight of these four observations can make it very difficult for the average Christian in America to know how to respond to the rise of global extremists while at the same time trying to genuinely love Islamic friends, neighbors, and co-workers. There are a handful of

---

[155] James A. Beverley, *Nelson's Illustrated Guide to Religions: A Comprehensive Introduction to the Religions of the World*, 270-271.

[156] James A. Beverley, *Nelson's Illustrated Guide to Religions: A Comprehensive Introduction to the Religions of the World*, 259-260.

reminders that might be helpful as we try to have a balanced approach as Christians.

First, the policies of our country were never designed to advance the Great Commission. This is the purpose of the church and not the state. The calling of the Christian is to win people for Christ, whereas our country is designed to provide for and protect its citizens. Although our country was established upon the firm foundation of a Judeo-Christian worldview, our calling as Christians will sometimes differ from the viewpoint of our country.

Second, it is noble for any country to treat the citizens of the world with dignity and respect. In God's command to the nation of Israel, He urged them "to do justice, to love kindness, and to walk humbly with your God (Micah 6:8)." Although this was a direct command for the nation of Israel, it is a helpful model for countries that wish to express genuine dignity to both citizens and foreigners within its borders. Throughout the Old Testament, God gave very clear instructions on how to care for everyone who lived within its borders (Leviticus 19). At the very least, our country should attempt to model this kind of compassion for the needy and deprived within our world.

Finally, the challenge for the Christian is to recognize that the church's role is fundamentally different than the role of the government. We have been asked by Jesus to go into all the world and preach the gospel (Matthew 28:18-20). As part of our cultural mandate to care for all of humanity, we have been asked to express love and compassion for people of all nationalities, cultures, and religions. Specifically, we must remember that God has called us to love and communicate the gospel to those Muslims who live in peace in our neighborhoods and cities.

In my previous book, I suggested a number of ways that Christians can better connect with Muslim friends, co-workers, or neighbors. Here are some suggestions that may be helpful:

- Surround your Muslim friends with unconditional acts of love. Care for them, support them, and be willing to be part of their lives. Invite them to your house, enjoy joint activities with your children, or participate in city-wide events.

- Don't be afraid to have discussions about your faith and spiritual things. Muslims, and especially those from other countries, often see American Christians as cold, secular, and undisciplined. Seeing a Christian who is openly captivated by Jesus can be a big eye-opener.
- Pray for your Muslim friends. Muslims are very responsive to the supernatural. Pray that the Lord would speak to your Muslim friend through the Holy Spirit. There are many modern-day examples of Muslims who came to Christ through dreams and visions.
- If talking about spiritual things, by all means read the Scriptures to your Muslim friend. Show that you hold the Word of God in the greatest regard and that your theology stems from it.
- If you are asking Muslims about their faith, avoid talking about the concept of Jihad. Muslims are tired of non-Muslims only wanting to talk about the concept of Jihad with them when they discuss Islam. Imagine if the only thing your non-Christian friends ever wanted to discuss with you was the Crusades. That's how Muslims feel.

It's perfectly appropriate for a Christian to embrace political positions designed to keep our country safe. However, as a follower of Jesus Christ we should keep the salvation of Muslims as our primary concern.

TIMELESS TRUTHS FOR A CULTURE THAT TEXTS

We must strike a balance between expressing unconditional love to Islamic friends and neighbors as Christians and protecting our country as a citizen. It's the tension between embracing peaceful Muslims and combating radical extremists.

Question 47
How Important is the Difference between Protestants and Catholics?

On October 31, 1517, Martin Luther, who was a Catholic monk, posted the ninety-five theses, which he had composed in Latin, on the door of *All Saints' Church* in Wittenberg. He addressed major issues within the Roman Catholic Church. They were not trivial issues or minor doctrines. The issues were so important that the Roman Catholic Church was split; this split is known as the Protestant Reformation.

The position of the Reformers regarding justification (grace alone, faith alone) was so radical that it was pronounced as an anathema by the Roman Catholic Council of Trent in 1547. In 1994, in an attempt to minimize the wide doctrinal gap that separates evangelicalism and Roman Catholicism, a document entitled "Evangelicals and Catholics Together: The Christian Mission in the Third Millennium," was signed by a number of prominent evangelicals. Although praised by many, it was also resisted by many prominent evangelical leaders, including the highly regarded teacher and author, John MacArthur, who has had grave concerns about this effort:

> Both of these men surely understand the gulf that divides Roman Catholicism from the evangelical faith. It is not a philosophical or political difference, but a theological one. And it is not a matter of trivia. The key difference between evangelicalism and Roman Catholicism is a difference over the gospel. The issues that separated the Reformers from the Roman Catholic Church go to the heart of what evangelicals believe about salvation.[157]

As we think about the 500-year-old historic difference between Protestants and the Catholic Church, it's helpful to remember that over two billion people call themselves Christians, and that Catholics comprise roughly one-half of that number. Over the years, they have

---

[157] John MacArthur, *Evangelicals and Catholics Together*, http://www.gty.org/resources/articles/A149/evangelicals-and-catholics-together.

ɔeen represented by iconic individuals such as Pope John Paul II and Mother Theresa. In addition, it's important to recognize that Catholics and Protestants hold a tremendous deal in common. Both groups embrace the following central beliefs of the Christian faith:

- God as Sovereign Creator
- Trinity
- Incarnation of Christ and the Virgin Birth
- Christ's atonement for the sins of mankind
- Bodily resurrection of Christ
- Future judgment
- Heaven and hell

In addition to these core doctrines, many of the most powerful voices for a return to morality in our country have come from leading Catholic intellectuals and from the Catholic Church itself. When no one else was publicly standing against abortion, the Catholic Church never wavered.

Despite these similarities, one of the single biggest issues that forever divided the church was the answer to this single question, "How is a person made righteous before God?" The Protestant reformers answered, by "grace alone, faith alone" while the Catholic Church answered, by "grace through the sacraments." The Roman Catholic Church insisted that the reformers were heretics. In addition, the church insisted that the sacraments were absolutely necessary for a person to be righteous before God.

The issue of how a person becomes right in the eyes of God is not simply an issue of history. It still has great importance for people who are directly or indirectly connected to the Catholic Church. Allow me to illustrate this by once again telling you the story of my good friend Jason. He is a non-practicing Catholic who is unabashed in his belief in God, the trustworthiness of the Bible, absolute morality, and the reality of the afterlife—both heaven and hell. Jason's background places him in an ideal position to understand and appreciate the sacrifice of Christ on the cross. However, like many Catholics, Jason is still uncertain about exactly how a person becomes right in the eyes of God (e.g. gets to heaven). Recently, when I asked him about how a person begins a relationship with God, he hesitated for a couple of minutes before admitting that he wasn't quite sure. Many Catholics focus too much of their attention on what it takes to be a good Catholic. Jason is not unique in his confusion on exactly how a person begins his relationship with God. Fortunately, he is still open to talking about the implications of the gospel of Jesus Christ. Jason, like many Catholics, could benefit from the simple illustration that I call the "Dot Approach" and the "Line Approach."

The Protestant view uses what I call the "Dot Approach." This approach emphasizes that a person at a single point in time (signified by a dot) is declared righteous by God based upon a genuine affirmation that Jesus Christ died in their place on the cross and that He will be the Lord of their life. At this moment, a person is given the righteousness of Christ (Romans 4:22; 10:9-10), and this allows us to be truly saved. We are saved by God's Grace at the precise point that we express genuine faith in the sacrifice of Christ on the cross. God does something that we are incapable of doing for ourselves. This approach reflects the historic claims by the Protestant Reformation that "we are saved by grace alone, by faith alone (Ephesians 2:8)"

The Catholic view uses what I call the "Line Approach." Imagine for a moment that we are now looking at a horizontal line. Catholics don't emphasize becoming righteous at a single point in time. They believe that God's righteousness is infused (poured into the soul sacramentally). In other words, a person must cooperate with this infused righteousness throughout his or her lifetime. The sacraments carry God's grace to the Christian. Think of them as a container. If you want to have God's grace, He has provided the sacraments of the Catholic Church to carry or administer them. By accepting the seven sacraments (Baptism, Confirmation, Eucharist, Penance, Matrimony, Holy Orders, and the Anointing of the Sick) that the Roman Catholic Church offers, a person receives the necessary grace of God to maintain a righteous life. These sacraments are essential for salvation.

Unfortunately, the most tragic development within the Catholic Church is that far too many Catholics seem to be quite unaware of the central component of Christian salvation. Peter Kreeft, a Catholic professor at Boston College, has witnessed firsthand the rampant confusion about the essence of justification. Listen to two of his observations:

> At Heaven's gate our entrance ticket, according to Scripture and Church dogma, is not our good works or our sincerity, but our faith, which glues us to Jesus. He saves us; we do not save ourselves. But I find, incredibly, that 9 out of 10 Catholics do not know this, the absolutely central, core, essential dogma of Christianity. Protestants are right: most Catholics do, in fact, believe a whole other religion. Well over 90% of students I have polled who have had 12 years of catechism classes, even Catholic high schools, say they expect to go to Heaven because they tried, or did their best, or had compassionate feelings to everyone, or were sincere. They hardly ever mention Jesus.[158]
>
> Many Catholics, to this day, have learned the Catholic and biblical doctrine. They think we are saved by good intentions or being nice or sincere or trying a little harder or doing a sufficient number of good deeds. Over the past twenty-five years I have asked hundreds of Catholic college students the question: If you should die tonight and God asks you why he should let you into heaven, what would you answer? The vast majority of them simply do not know the right answer to this, the most important of all questions, the very essence of Christianity. They usually do not even mention Jesus![159]

The observations by Kreeft are insightful. It is absolutely crucial that we make sure that Catholic family and friends are absolutely certain of the path to salvation. It's vital that we use the "dot approach" and "line approach" to clarify the means of being made righteous in the presence of God. It is our obligation and calling to clarify the essence of the gospel message to everyone who might not understand it.

The importance of navigating the differences between Protestants and Catholics is a very personal issue for me. Although I was raised in a solid evangelical church, my paths have repeatedly crossed with many Catholics—both devout and non-practicing. I have had long conversations with family members, close friends, and associates who

---

158 Peter Kreeft, http://www.peterkreeft.com/topics/hauled-aboard.htm

159 Peter Kreeft, http://www.catholiceducation.org/en/religion-and-philosophy/apologetics/justification-by-faith.html

were either raised in a Catholic home, were once Catholic, or have converted to Catholicism. My good friend Derick (who was introduced earlier in the book) is a perfect example of the care that is needed when discussing this issue. Although Derick was raised in a Christian house (Protestant and non-Catholic), he married into a Catholic family and was immediately thrust into walking the fine line of what he believes while respecting the viewpoints of family members. Like Kreeft, Derick is concerned about Catholics who just follow the sacraments in the hopes that their religious service will guarantee their entrance into heaven. He questions the cavalier approach to sin by far too many Catholics who think that as long as they confess their sin to the priest, everything is okay. Derick's life story is an important reminder that how we discuss these issues and how we interact with our Catholic family and friends makes all the difference in the world.

Of course, it's important to remember that Catholics are a very diverse group. Some Catholics view their salvation the same way as Protestants. They don't view the Sacraments (good works) as necessary for salvation. Some Catholics are predominately guided by their trust and faith in Jesus as their Savior. Although their church pronounces certain truths that differ from the Bible, they exercise simple and childlike faith in that they trust Christ alone for their salvation. Unfortunately, too many Catholics seem to exhibit ignorance of the biblical path to heaven.

I mention the diversity within the Catholic Church to make sure that we don't prematurely critique a person's faith or the outcome of their salvation. It is impossible to look inside the heart of a person and determine whether or not they are relying exclusively on the sacrifice of Christ on the cross for their salvation. We will never be able to make that assessment. We can declare the gospel. We can clarify the gospel. However, we can't judge the precise status of person's relationship with God merely by looking on the outside.

Martin Luther clearly believed that the essence of the Christian gospel is the declaration of the righteousness of Christ on behalf of the Christian. He believed that the Christian can rejoice at being declared righteous by God at a single point in time. Luther expressed it with these words:

> And this is the confidence that Christians have and our real joy of conscience, that by faith our sins become no longer ours but Christ's upon whom God placed the sins of all of us. He took upon himself our sins . . . . All the righteousness of Christ becomes ours. . . . He spreads his cloak and covers us.[160]

TIMELESS TRUTHS FOR A CULTURE THAT TEXTS

Christianity believes that a person is declared righteous before God by faith in Christ's death on the cross. We dare not add anything or subtract anything from this equation!

160 Martin Luther, *Explanations of the Ninety-five Theses* in Norman L. Geisler & Ralph E. MacKenzie, *Roman Catholics and Evangelicals Agreements and Differences* (Grand Rapids: Baker Books, 1995), 97-98.

Question 48
How Should Christians View Judaism?

The Ten Commandments is a 1956 film about the Egyptian Prince, Moses, who learns of his true heritage as a Hebrew and his divine mission as the deliverer of his people. This film, directed by Cecil B. Demille, has so many memorable moments, but none more powerful as when Pharaoh Seti I must banish his own adopted son (Moses) from himself and the kingdom of Egypt. If anyone has watched the movie they can probably still remember the words of the king, "Let the name of Moses be stricken from every book and tablet. Stricken from every pylon and obelisk of Egypt. Let the name of Moses be unheard and unspoken, erased from the memory of man, for all time."

The movie reminds us that Judaism is one of the world's oldest religions, featuring not only the iconic figure of Moses who received the 10 Commandments from God on Mount Sinai, but extending back nearly 2000 years before Christ when God called Abraham to leave his home and follow Him.

Unlike any other religion, Judaism forms the theological and historical foundation for everything that is fully realized within the Christian faith. Alister McGrath describes the unique solidarity between Judaism and Christianity:

> What have Christians inherited from the Jews? Everything in the Old Testament: the knowledge of the true God. Comparing that knowledge with the knowledge of all the other religions of the world is like comparing sunlight with fog. Six crucial and distinctive concepts stand out: monotheism, creation, law, redemption, sin, and faith.[161]

The two religions share the same historical foundation found in the Old Testament. The two religions also share the same belief in one Almighty and Sovereign God who created the universe. Together we share a

---

[161] Alister McGrath, *Fundamentals of the Faith: Essays in Christian Apologetics*, 81.

reverence for the Scriptures, a commitment to biblical morality, and a belief in the special relationship between the nation of Israel and God. We also mutually acknowledge God's redemptive work through the sacrificial system of Israel, prophetic statements about the Messiah, and our reverence for the nature of God. All of these are based upon the truths found in the Old Testament.

Before we attempt to clarify some of the more profound differences between these two religions, it's important to make a big disclaimer. Judaism is a very diverse religion that embraces a wide range of beliefs. Many Jews are secular in their orientation. They respect the cultural heritage of being a Jew, yet have a very secular worldview that embraces relativity and anti-supernaturalism. Religious Jews generally fall into three camps: orthodox, conservative, and reform. Orthodox Judaism embraces the 613 commands found in the teaching of the Torah (first five books of the Bible). Orthodox Jews have a strict understanding of moral, cultural, and dietary issues. Conservative Judaism seeks to preserve Jewish tradition and ritual but has a more flexible approach to the interpretation of the law than Orthodox Judaism. The leadership of Conservative Judaism is strongly committed to ensuring that the next generation of Conservative Jews continues to lead an authentic Jewish lifestyle. Although they believe in the divine origin of the Old Testament laws, they also affirm the role of scientific biblical criticism. Reformed Judaism denies that the Torah or the Talmud is the revelation of God. In light of this belief, reformed Jews attempt to decide which religious laws apply in the modern world.

As we compare the historic perspectives of Conservative and Orthodox Judaism with the historic claims of Christianity, it is clear there are a handful of profound differences. The first and most important difference between Christianity and Judaism is the Person of Jesus Christ. Christianity teaches that Jesus was God in the flesh (John 1:1, 14; Hebrews 1:8) while Judaism strongly denies that Jesus was God in the flesh. Since the inception of the church, many Jews continue to reject Jesus as the Son of God (John 1:11; 5:18; 6:41-42).

Christianity teaches that Jesus Christ is the fulfillment of the Old Testament prophecies of a coming Messiah and Savior (Isaiah 7:14;9:6-7; Micah 5:2). There are over 300 prophecies in the Hebrew Scriptures that provide many details that were true of Jesus of Nazareth. Here is a brief overview of several of these predictions:

- Messiah was predicted to be born at Bethlehem (Micah 5:2).
- Messiah was predicted to be from the tribe of Judah (Genesis 49:10).
- Messiah would present himself by riding on a donkey (Zechariah 9:9).
- Messiah would be tortured to death (Psalm 22:14-18).
- Messiah would arrive before the destruction of the Second Temple (Daniel 9:24-27).
- Messiah experienced suffering, silence at his trial, death, and burial in the rich man's tomb (Isaiah 52:13-53:12).

Although Judaism recognizes Jesus as a good teacher, it does not believe that Jesus was the Messiah. Jews believe that the Messiah will be a human, non-divine person who will restore the physical kingdom of Israel, rebuild the temple in Jerusalem and bring earthly peace. Although Jesus did not immediately fulfill these specific objectives the Scripture teaches that He will accomplish these in His second coming (Revelation 19:11-19; Matthew 24:31; Zechariah 12:10-14).

Christianity fulfills and completes the message of the Old Testament. We embrace the completed revelation of God (Hebrews 1:1-2), the revelation of the predicted Messiah (John 1:41), and the full understanding of righteousness by grace through faith (Romans 3:21-25; 5:8-9; Galatians 2:16).

The other profound difference between the two faiths resides in the manner in which a person is accepted in the sight of a morally perfect God. Christianity has historically taught that believers are granted the righteousness of Christ solely by grace through faith (Ephesians 2:8-9). In the Old Testament, the people of Israel had to offer sincere prayers of repentance, turn away from their sin and offer appropriate sacrifices in order to receive forgiveness from their sins. By the time that the early church was begun, the beliefs and actions of Rabbinic Jews in the first century was clearly different than the Christian message preached by the Apostles (Acts 4:12; Romans 3:19-24). Rabbinic Judaism saw the faith of Abraham (Genesis 15:6) as a meritorious act. They exchanged the word "merit" for righteousness and rendered the concept "merit of faith." Faith, in historic Judaism, was seen as embracing both the fundamental belief in the one God and also the way of life that corresponds to this belief.

The central message of the Apostle Paul in Romans is that people were never saved by the works of the Law. Paul clearly says, "For what does the Scripture say? 'And Abraham believed God, and it was reckoned to him as righteousness (Romans 4:3)'". God imputed or credited righteousness to Abraham's account in such a way that he could actually stand before a perfect, loving God. King David understood and experienced the same wonderful gift of forgiveness and salvation (Romans 4:6-8). The message of Christianity is that Old Testament and New Testament saints are saved by God's grace through faith (Romans 4:3; 6:23; Ephesians 2:8-9). Of course, the uniqueness of the New Testament age is that the object of a person's faith has been narrowed around the person of Jesus Christ. The faith of the believer in the Old Testament was focused generally upon a person's belief in God's provision of His righteousness (Genesis 15:6; Romans 4:3).

Judaism and Christianity have a shared history. Although Christians have not always treated Jews with dignity and respect, our theological underpinnings come from the same source—the revealed will of God in the Old Testament. Everything in the Old Testament was designed to describe the necessity of a blood sacrifice to atone for the sins of each Jew (Exodus 12:27; Leviticus 16). The New Testament describes God's ultimate and permanent (once for all) plan to atone for the sins of the entire world. Jesus, who was the predicted Messiah and Lamb of God (John 1:29), would offer Himself as the definitive and perfect sacrifice to God (1 Peter 1:19). Ultimately, it comes down to a person's view of Jesus Christ. Is He God in the flesh who died on the cross for the sins of the world or not?

TIMELESS TRUTHS FOR A CULTURE THAT TEXTS

All religions are defined by their opinion about the person of Christ. Judaism fails to recognize Jesus as the coming Messiah and as the perfect sacrifice for the sins of the world.

Question 49
How Do You Compare Christianity with Buddhism?

One of the most revered religious persons in our world is the Dalai Lama. People universally recognize him as a man of peace, wisdom, and kindness—everything that people in our culture would expect from a religious leader. It's easy to see the Dalai Lama's attraction due to his charisma, insight, and humility. The Dalai Lama is also admired because he espouses a level of religious tolerance and inclusion that people in the modern world greatly value. In an interview with religious expert James Beverley, the Dalai Lama stated very clearly his views on other religions:

> 'Changing religion is not easy,' he said, 'Sometimes it creates more confusion.' If someone in the West finds Buddhism more suitable, 'it is their individual right, but it is extremely important to keep their respect towards their own traditional religion.'[162]

> To some people Christianity is much more effective, in some other case, Islam, Judaism, Hinduism, or Zorastrianism. . . . Even if I say that Buddhism is the best, that everybody should follow Buddhism, everybody is not going to become a Buddhist. . . . I can say that for me personally, Buddhism is best because the Buddhist approach is most effective to me.[163]

As I've mentioned in various sections of this book, all religions are not equally true. Buddhism is very different from the major world religions. In fact, Christianity differs significantly from Buddhism. Christianity believes in a personal God who is omnipresent, omniscient, holy, and who created the universe. Christians believe people are sinful, that there is a coming judgment, and in the afterlife in heaven or hell. On the other hand, Buddhism denies all of these beliefs. The ultimate reality (God) is impersonal, the world is uncreated, and life's ultimate goal is not personal immortality. The concepts of sin and salvation play no role

---

[162] James A. Beverley, *Nelson's Illustrated Guide to Religions*, 65.

[163] James A. Beverley, *Nelson's Illustrated Guide to Religions*, 66.

within the religion of Buddhism. Let's briefly investigate two of the more troubling issues of Buddhism.

First, the Buddhist position on karma has dangerous implications. In one of his books, the Dalai Lama expressed that a person killed by a lightning bolt earned that fate by committing a misdeed in a previous life. Few people believe that this is the fate of people in life—that they are tortured and mistreated for sins/misdeeds in a previous life. It's hard to believe that the horrific rape of Buddhist nuns by Communist soldiers during the purge of Tibet was a part of their debt to karma. If these horrible events are the earned fate of a person from a previous lifetime, does this excuse the person who inflicted the torture? We can't expect society to penalize the darker elements of humanity if we truly believe that people are simply getting what they deserved as a result of acts committed in a previous life. Karma and reincarnation are terribly flawed as they relate to explaining the presence of evil and personal responsibility in this life. The simple truth is that Jesus never taught such a callous and unreasonable position. When Jesus was asked the reason for a tower falling on innocent bystanders, Jesus clearly stated that no one was guilty (Luke 13:1-5). In other words, there are certain things that simply happen in a fallen world due to the evil choices of people or the interaction of natural forces within our planet.

The Buddhist position on karma also has terrifying implications for a person's perception of God. Is it really fair and good for God to continue to keep score of the sins of a previous lifetime? The Christian view of God is entirely built upon the concept of grace (Ephesians 2:8-9; Hebrews 4:16). Although people have sinned and are flawed, God unilaterally sent Christ to the cross to offer every single person the opportunity to receive salvation. This offer of salvation involves God's ability to overlook any sin from this lifetime—the only lifetime for which a person can reasonably be held accountable.

Finally, the notion of karma is totally inconsistent with the sacrificial death of Christ on the cross. Did Jesus deserve to die? Was his death on the cross part of karma from his previous life? Clearly, the concept of karma is absolutely inconsistent with a reasonable view of the reasons for evil but also for the sacrifice of Christ on the cross.

Unlike the historical evidence for the reliability of the Bible, the historical integrity of the earliest documents about Buddha pales in significance. The earliest documents about the life of Buddha were written four or five centuries after the death of Guatama Buddha. James Beverley cites the insight of a devout Buddhist scholar as a strong indictment about the historical reliability of these documents:

> In *A Short History of Buddhism*, Edward Conze, a devout Buddhist scholar, dismisses any 'confident assertions' about what the Buddha really said as 'mere guesswork.' Conze wrote in the introduction to *Buddhist Scriptures*: 'Buddhists possess nothing that corresponds to the New Testament.'[164]

It seems that one of the core tests of a religion is whether or not something actually happened in history. We can't ask people to believe in the tenants of a world view when it is doubtful whether it dovetails with real events in history. History continues to be a helpful gauge by which we evaluate the truthfulness of religious worldviews. It is still very important to determine if what a religion's founder claimed to have said is, in fact, what he said. If there is credible evidence that Buddha didn't even utter these words, a person will struggle in making the reasonable claim that those are the positions or claims of Buddha.

TIMELESS TRUTHS FOR A CULTURE THAT TEXTS

Karma cannot explain final judgment, sacrifice of Christ on the cross, or the reality of evil. It fails to explain these truths.

---

[164] James A. Beverley, *Nelson's Illustrated Guide to Religions*, 88-89.

Question 50
Does the Teaching of Hinduism Reflect Truth?

Religion professors and skeptics enjoy using the story of the four blind men who discover an elephant. Since the men have never encountered an elephant, they grope about, seeking to understand and describe this new phenomenon. One grasps the trunk and concludes it is a snake. Another explores one of the elephant's legs and describes it as a tree. A third finds the elephant's tail and announces that it is a rope. And the fourth blind man, after discovering the elephant's side, concludes that it is, after all, a wall. Each in his blindness is describing the same thing: an elephant. Yet each describes the same thing in a very different way.

According to many, this story illustrates the different religions of the world. Although all religions are describing God from their unique perspective, they seem to believe they are talking about the same God. In our politically correct culture, Hinduism, is often represented as being the most tolerant and accepting of other faiths because they seem to embrace the principle found in the story of the four blind men.

Religious expert James Beverley describes it this way, "Hindus believe that no particular religion teaches the only way to salvation above all others, but that all genuine religious paths are facets of God's Pure Love and Light, deserving tolerance and understanding."[165] Gandhi is the most famous Hindu of modern times. He defended the independence of India and the rights of those who are deemed unclean (Untouchables) within the Indian culture, and worked for peaceful Muslim-Hindu relations. As a result, many of the socially elite and opinion shapers of our modern culture are drawn to the tolerance that is embodied by Hinduism, which is the third largest religion of the world.

It's important to remind the reader, as I have in other places within this book, that those who claim that all religions are the same or true are simply misinformed or disingenuous.

---

[165] James A. Beverley, *Nelson's Illustrated Guide to Religions*, 173.

If it is simply not reasonable to believe that all religions are equally true. We must come to grips with the singular fact that truth by definition is exclusive. Certain things are true and certain things are false. Certain religions are right while others are wrong. It doesn't mean that everything they teach is wrong or that they don't have a positive impact on their adherents. It simply means that we must test the truth claims of any religion before we place our trust in it. Once again Zacharias correctly places his finger on the issue:

> If the test demonstrates truth then we are morally compelled to believe it. And this is precisely the point from which many are trying to run. As G.K. Chesterton said, the problem with Christianity is not that it has been tried and found wanting, but that it has been found difficult and left untried.[166]

As we begin to evaluate whether or not Hinduism accurately depicts the truth concerning God and reality, it can be very helpful to remind people of the inherent weaknesses of Hinduism as a worldview. After all, the ultimate hope of any religion is to reassure its adherents that its views dovetail with reality. There is little doubt that many of the tenets of Hinduism help its adherents achieve a greater sense of personal peace and achievement. However, if the core foundation of Hinduism simply doesn't pass the reality test, then it can hardly convince people that it is the ultimate expression of truth. I've taken the liberty of adapting some of the observations by noted Christian apologist Peter Kreeft.

WEAKNESS #1: HINDUISM DOES NOT BELIEVE IN ONE SUPREME GOD

Hinduism is pantheistic. It teaches that the world is part of God and that humans share in the divine reality which is God. Hinduism believes in thousands of gods and goddesses, although they have historically venerated Brahma, Vishnu, and Shiva. Most Hindus don't believe in a personal and objectively real God who is distinct from all creation. In contrast, Christianity claims there is one supreme being (Deuteronomy

---

[166] Ravi Zacharias, http://rzim.org/a-slice-of-infinity/point-of-exclusion.

6:4; 1 Timothy 2:5) who brought the universe into existence out of nothing (Genesis 1:1; John 1:1).

Of course, if God brought the world into existence, then believers in the Hinduistic viewpoint must explain their view of the origin of the universe. Hinduism believes that the universe undergoes endless cycles of creation and dissolution. However, at the same time, Hindus assert that the universe was created 311,040 billion years ago even though there is little explanation for how or who brought the universe into existence. This seems to be in contrast with scientific evidence that the universe came into existence at a single point in time as a result of the Big Bang approximately 13 to 20 billion years ago. In light of this, the Hindu assertion seems far-fetched and arbitrary. In addition, it leaves a person to wonder what entity was the driving force behind the beginning of the universe. Christianity believes that the best explanation is that the universe had a finite beginning approximately 13+ billion years ago caused by a transcendent and personal being who stood outside of creation. Hinduism has literally thousands of gods and no clear proposal for who or what brought the world into existence.

WEAKNESS #2: HINDUISM BELIEVES IN REINCARNATION

One of the foundational and uncompromising tenets of Hinduism is the doctrine of reincarnation. Beverley describes the teaching this way:

> Hindus believe in karma, the law of cause and effect by which each individual creates his own destiny by his thoughts, words, and deeds. Hindus believe that the soul reincarnates, evolving through many births until all karmas have been resolved, and moksha, spiritual knowledge and liberation from the cycle of rebirth, is attained. Not a single soul will be eternally deprived of this destiny.[167]

This is a huge departure from historic Christianity, which states that everyone will face eternal judgment after our life on earth is finished

---

[167] James A. Beverley, *Nelson's Illustrated Guide to Religions*, 173.

(Hebrews 9:27). Furthermore, the Scripture indicates that one's destiny is only determined by the individual free choice of a person (John 3:16; John 20:30-31), and not the endless cycle of reincarnations that purge an individual's soul.

In addition to the tension between reincarnation and the teaching of Scripture, there is the very real tension between the logical and philosophical implications of reincarnation. If life is an endless cycle of reincarnations, when did it all start? If life is an endless cycle of reincarnations, how is there an end when a person finally attains spiritual knowledge and liberation from the cycle of rebirth? Ravi Zacharias expresses the difficulty this way:

> Philosopher William Lane Craig reminds us that an infinite regress of causes is like trying to jump out of a bottomless pit. How do you start if you never reach the bottom? On the other hand, one might well ask, if every birth is a rebirth, what karma was paid for in his first birth?[168]

WEAKNESS #3: HINDUISM DENIES THE REALITY OF EVIL

The existence of good and evil cannot exist without a transcendent moral law given to humanity by a morally perfect God. The difficulty with Hinduism is that it has no clear answer to the problem of suffering. Think about it this way. If everything in the physical world is not real and is, instead, illusory, why should a person believe that anything is evil? Why should a person complain when something evil is done against them? The Hindu view of life is simply not consistent with our view of the world around us. Every single day people make decisions, good and bad, based upon the belief that what surrounds them is truly happening and is genuinely real. Hinduism paints a very different picture of our world—a picture that people don't truly believe makes senses. Ravi Zacharias tells a funny story to illustrate the inherent inconsistency of the Hindu position:

---

[168] Ravi Zacharias, *Jesus Among Other Gods: The Absolute Claims of the Christian Message* (Nashville: Word Publishing, 2000), 122.

> India's leading philosopher, Shankara just finished lecturing the king on the deception of the mind and his delusion of material reality. The next day, the king let loose an elephant that went on a rampage, and Shankara ran up a tree to find safety. When the king asked him why he ran if the elephant was non-real, Shankara, not to be outdone, said, "What the king actually saw was a non-real me climbing up a non-real tree!" One might add, "That is a non-real answer."[169]

WEAKNESS #4: HINDUISM DOES NOT BELIEVE IN ABSOLUTE MORALITY

Hinduism believes that God is in everything. He is inherently linked to everything good and everything evil in the world. Of course, this means that in the Hinduistic worldview there is no absolute morality and no divine being who has established a clear right and wrong in the world. However, the best explanation for the clear moral absolutes of our world (murder is wrong, rape is wrong, genocide is wrong, etc.) is the existence of a moral lawgiver. The God of the Bible is a morally perfect being who has established His divine will and morality as the standard by which the world ought to operate.

Consistent with their denial of absolute morality, Hindus don't believe there is a need for a personal savior to atone for a person's sin. Hinduism believes that the ultimate goal in life is to fully realize one's union and relationship with god. However, if a person's definition of God does not include the concept of morality, then it is clear that there would be no need for a remedy for personal moral failure (sin) in the form of a savior.

WEAKNESS #5: HINDUISM DENIES FREE WILL

One of the foundational realities in the Western world and within the truths taught in the Bible is that every single person has been granted the dignity of free will (John 3:16; Matthew 23:37; Luke 22:21-22). Although God is sovereign He has created this world in such a way that

---

[169] Ravi Zacharias, *Jesus Among Other Gods: The Absolute Claims of the Christian Message*, 119

people can make choices entirely by themselves. Kreeft describes the dangerous implications of Hinduism:

> The word spoken by God himself as his own essential name, the word I, is the ultimate illusion, not the ultimate reality, according to the East. There is no separate ego; all is one. Because individuality is illusion, so is free will. If free will is illusion, so is sin. And if sin is illusion, so is hell. Perhaps the strongest attraction of Eastern religions is in their denial of sin, guilt, and hell. Thus the two essential points of Christianity, sin and salvation, are both missing in the East. If there is no sin, no salvation is needed, only enlightenment. We need not be born again, only to wake up to our innate divinity. If I am part of God, I can never be really alienated from God by sin.[170]

Some of the concepts of Hinduism sound lofty and mystical until a person attempts to apply them to real life. Remember, if everything is illusion then nothing that happens is real and events should have no negative impact upon a person. If I want to steal the laptop from a fellow student who is a Hindu he or she should have no problem with my decision because it is all an illusion. If we look around the world and see rampant terrorism, why do we attempt to rally the powers of the world to stop it if it is all an illusion? The simple truth is that our world is not an illusion. God has granted each of us the dignity of free will and the clear awareness of moral right and wrong.

TIMELESS TRUTHS FOR A CULTURE THAT TEXTS

To insist that all of life is an illusion is to deny the most basic of realities in the modern world—the dignity of free will.

---

170 Peter Kreeft, *Fundamentals of the Faith: Essays in Christian Apologetics*, 91.

About the Author
Dr. Brent Strawsburg
President of Brent Strawsburg Apologetics

Introduction

Dr. Strawsburg has served in ministry for over thirty years, pastoring two different churches. During this time, he utilized apologetics in every aspect of ministry—on college campuses, when equipping others, during outreach efforts, and when preaching on apologetic topics from the pulpit. Dr. Brent has studied with some of the sharpest minds in the United States and can teach apologetics in a way that is accessible to everyone in the church. Dr. Brent is a highly sought after speaker for churches and conferences. He has a unique ability to make every apologetic topic accessible and practical for every single person in attendance. He received a Master of Divinity from Talbot School of Theology, a Master of Arts in Christian Apologetics from Biola University, and a Doctor of Ministry from Dallas Theological Seminary.

Non-Profit Status

Dr. Brent Strawsburg is Founder and President of Brent Strawsburg Apologetics (BSA), which specializes in making apologetics relevant for the church. BSA is a registered 501(c)(3) non-profit whose mission is "Using Christian Apologetics to Shape Culture, Strengthen Faith & Empower Witness."

Speaking Topics

The following are some of the topics that Dr. Strawsburg is able to address:

- How to Disarm Your Doubts
- How to Talk to Skeptics
- Why Does God Allow Evil & Suffering?
- Where is God When It Hurts?
- How Can Faith Survive a Relativistic Culture?
- Is Belief in God Reasonable?

- CAN YOU TRUST THE BIBLE?
- THE RESURRECTION: MYTH OR MIRACLE?
- IS ETERNAL PUNISHMENT (HELL) FAIR?
- IS JESUS THE ONLY WAY TO GOD?
- FACING END-OF-LIFE ISSUES WITH A LOVED ONE
- IS MORMONISM CHRISTIAN?
- IS ISLAM OR CHRISTIANITY TRUE?
- HOMOSEXUALITY & SAME-SEX MARRIAGE

AVAILABLE RESOURCES

If Dr. Brent Strawsburg comes to your church, he will provide the following resources:

- Publicity for all messages/seminars
- Message notes or syllabus
- PowerPoint® presentations
- Insight/advice on strategies for incorporating apologetics within the church
- Apologetic resources

All of Dr. Brent's materials provide the highest quality graphics and technology to engage the listener throughout the presentation. Brent has assembled a team of gifted professionals to put together a syllabus and PowerPoint® presentation that accompanies every seminar/message. His website www.brentstrawsburg.com contains examples (PDF, PPT, MP3 Sound, and MP4 Video) of practical and engaging seminars and messages.

MINISTRY OPTIONS

Dr. Brent has been quite successful in offering a range of ministry options that effectively help churches to strengthen faith and empower witness. Here are some of the options:

Defending the Faith Conference: This format effectively rallies the entire church in order to focus on select apologetic topics. Dr. Brent offers two or three seminars over the weekend of the conference, culminating in a Sunday morning message. This effectively touches everyone within the church. The seminars provide in-depth and practical insight for those interested while also providing access to everyone on Sunday morning.

Weekend Seminars: This format features two or three seminars that address specific topics of interest to a church. These seminars can be offered on Friday night/Saturday morning, Saturday as a half-day event, or Saturday night.

Mid-week Seminars: This format uses a couple of evenings featuring one or two seminars per evening along with Q & A sessions.

Sunday Morning Messages: Churches sometimes place all the emphasis on addressing apologetic topics on Sunday morning. They commit to a single Sunday, back-to-back Sundays, or a regular schedule during which Dr. Brent returns to address key topics necessary to defend the Christian faith.

Church Conferences: Groups like Mission ConneXion (Pacific Northwest) utilize BSA in addressing apologetic topics in their apologetic track seminars during their two-day conference. This approach can work for denominational, mission, or equipping/evangelism conferences.

COST

Dr. Strawsburg will come to your church for a very reasonable cost (transportation, housing, and honorarium). Upon request he can supply your church with a document detailing his speaking fees.

CONTACT

Dr. Strawsburg can be contacted in the following ways:

Brent Strawsburg Apologetics
11462 Martha Ann Drive
Rossmoor, CA 90720
714-393-1823
www.brentstrawsburg.com
Brent.strawsburg@gmail.com

52591709R00133

Made in the USA
Lexington, KY
17 September 2019